NEW OLD
Designing for our future selves
Edited by Jeremy Myerson

the
DESIGN
MUSEUM

The NEW OLD exhibition is generously
supported by the Helen Hamlyn Trust and
AXA PPP healthcare with additional support
from Arthritis Research UK.

This publication, which accompanies the
exhibition, is supported by Arthritis Research UK
and the Helen Hamlyn Trust.

 THE HELEN HAMLYN TRUST

 ARTHRITIS
RESEARCH UK

 PPP HEALTHCARE
redefining / healthcare

NEW OLD
Contents

Foreword
Deyan Sudjic

Helen Hamlyn, through the trust that bears her name, has played
a key part in transforming the way the design world understands
how we can address the complex issues of ageing. She was behind
the Boilerhouse Project's pioneering exhibition in 1986, which
encouraged a group of leading designers to explore how simple
objects that facilitate daily living could be better shaped.
Specifically, the exhibition focused on the needs of people who
did not conform to what was then regarded as the human norm: the
vast number of individuals without the agility, stamina and eyesight
of a 30-year-old. The designers looked at how cutlery could
accommodate fingers shaped by arthritis and at how showers
could allow the unsteady to use them safely.

These issues – if they were addressed at all – were
conventionally treated in a utilitarian way rather than as part of
the mainstream language of design. The Design Museum, with the
generous support of the Helen Hamlyn Trust, AXA PPP healthcare
and Arthritis Research UK, returns to the theme of ageing three
decades later. If the idea of exploring design issues around age was
far-sighted in 1986, it is even more so today. We now find the entire
meaning of age transformed. Life expectancy has increased almost
everywhere, and for almost every social and ethnic group. This is
both a triumph for society, and a fundamental challenge to the way
that cultures organize themselves. How we can afford to support
the extended retirement that so many of us can now expect,
and potential tensions between an ageing – and often affluent –
generation and a less financially secure younger one, are just two
among many challenges.

The issues involved reflect fundamental and far-reaching
cultural concerns that manifest themselves differently in different
contexts. Japan, one of the world's most ethnically homogenous
industrial nations, appears reluctant to import migrants to care
for its rapidly ageing population. As a result, it is a pioneer in the
use of robotics in personal care.

In Western consumer society, it is becoming commonplace for fashion brands to use people who would once have simply been described as 'the old', to create their identity. We are also at a point when some of the billionaires of Silicon Valley are speculating about the possibility of extreme longevity with as much enthusiasm as their plans to reach Mars.

Where we live, how we live, how we support ourselves, and the quality of our lives as we age, represent the key questions that every society must address. They are questions that encompass medicine, economics, urbanism, technology and human behaviour. What connects them all, and makes them work for people's lives, is design. At the Design Museum, we understand design as a means of exploring and understanding the world. Design is sometimes about asking questions, as well as about answering them.

This book, and its sister exhibition, are trying to bring together the complex issues that shape the context for understanding ageing in our time and in the future. The book looks at new design approaches in response to the ageing process, bringing together new data and research. At the same time, in an echo of the 1986 exhibition, a range of leading designers of today have been invited to consider the questions raised by age and address them through the realization of a project.

These are issues that are as cultural as they are technical. Addressing them is a continuing process that is all about shaping attitudes as well as the way that societies do things.

Deyan Sudjic is Director of the Design Museum

The challenge of our time
Helen Hamlyn

As people live longer, we are looking at a future close at hand in which all developed societies will have more old people than young. This profound demographic shift has important implications for designers – if we want to enjoy the benefits of greater longevity and make those extra years healthier and happier, then we need to create new design solutions that respond to that challenge.

Thirty years ago, a principal concern was to design new products so that older people could continue to live independently in their own homes. This typically meant redesigning bathrooms, kitchens, furniture and lighting. Today, the focus is much broader – to enhance the experience of older age as people remain active in society and the workplace for longer. All types of design are required – from service and interaction design to fashion, transport and communication.

In 1986, when I organized the New Design for Old exhibition, my motivation was personal. My mother, then in her late 70s, needed support to live in her own apartment following an accident, but I discovered there was a dearth of well-designed products to help her.

I searched the market myself but was shocked and disappointed to find that no designers had properly considered simple innovations to make life easier for older people. On my fiftieth birthday, my husband Paul Hamlyn had given me the incredible gift of my own charitable foundation, and my first task was to think of ways to bring this issue to public attention.

Fortunately, I had studied at the Royal College of Art in London and many of the leading designers of the day were personal friends. So I tried to enlist their support. The first person I approached, the designer David Mellor, told me, 'If it was about children, I would do it.' My response was that children had designs galore before they were even a twinkle in their parents' eyes, but there was nothing for older people.

David Mellor thought about it and eventually agreed. He produced some fantastic cutlery for older people. Others became enthusiastic too, none more so than Terence Conran who offered his Boilerhouse gallery in the Victoria & Albert Museum, the forerunner to the Design Museum, to host the New Design for Old exhibition. Sixteen international designers produced new work for the show.

Looking back, I was surprised by how much influence the exhibition had. It was aimed at designers and the public, as well as manufacturers who were slow at picking up new and interesting ideas. It established a philosophy around designing for our future selves that would later underpin the establishment of a research centre in my name at the Royal College of Art. The Helen Hamlyn Centre for Design at the RCA has just celebrated its twenty-fifth anniversary.

The NEW OLD project at the Design Museum revisits that original exhibition, 30 years on. The Helen Hamlyn Trust is proud to support this initiative because it is important to understand how much has changed in demographic and technological terms in recent decades, how much will change over the next 30 years and how much design can contribute to making life better for ageing populations everywhere.

NEW OLD is an exhibition relevant for the time in which we live. My original exhibition was about products – the 2017 version is all about ideas. Approach it with an open mind.

Helen Hamlyn is a designer, philanthropist and the founder of The Helen Hamlyn Trust

Supporting healthier lives
Richard Turner

AXA PPP healthcare has a long history, dating back to before the foundation of the National Health Service, of protecting the health and well-being of our members. Over that time we have seen and adopted many health innovations, and those improvements have helped to increase our members' lifespans dramatically. There is no end in sight to this trend – the number of people in the UK aged 85 or more is expected to more than double in the next 25 years.

That is wonderful news for most of us, but it also brings new challenges. As our bodies and minds age, we become increasingly susceptible to different types of disease, including some that we cannot yet cure such as diabetes and dementia. But this is not a cause for despair. Our parents and grandparents faced greater health challenges with far less in the way of medical resources and knowledge to help them.

AXA is playing its part in funding research through the AXA Research Fund that was launched in 2007. AXA has so far invested €200m into the fund, sponsoring primary research across the world into the challenges facing humankind. These range from the causes of economic crashes, to better prediction of natural disasters, to improving human health. One researcher sponsored by the AXA Research Fund recently received a Nobel Prize for his work. Due to its importance, ageing has been a particular area of focus for the fund, and scientists and gerontologists are researching societal, economic and medical consequences and solutions. AXA PPP healthcare hopes to learn from this research and be an early implementer of findings, to benefit our members. AXA Research Fund results are freely available to all to use.

On 1 November 2016, the AXA PPP healthcare Group announced a long-term partnership with Age UK, the country's largest charity dedicated to helping everyone make the most of later life. While research is essential to tackle medical problems, we all face a range of challenges in life, and many of these challenges are better faced with help from people with first-hand practical experience. As part of the partnership, AXA has acquired Aid-Call Limited, Age UK's personal alarm service. Aid-Call provides AXA PPP healthcare with a foundation from which to expand beyond health solutions into holistic solutions – solutions that support people to live happier, safer and healthier lives.

However, there is one further element that is needed: design. Good design is the magic ingredient that transforms excellent, practical devices into desirable devices that people actually use. For example, personal alarms are used by more than one million people across the UK and regularly save lives. Many more people could benefit from these alarms but choose not to because this lifesaving service is seen as a symbol of ageing – it's a service that people need rather than want. We want to break that mould through better design and this is something we wish to bring to our new Aid-Call business.

Everyone should have the right to a happy, healthy, safe and secure life, no matter what age. The NEW OLD project stretches our imagination. It provides thought-provoking ideas and demonstrates how outstanding design can move a service from one that is necessary to one that is desired. We are excited to be sponsoring NEW OLD and hope that you find it equally inspiring.

Richard Turner is Strategy Director of AXA PPP healthcare

↑
Aura Power Suit by Yves Béhar, Fuseproject and Superflex
reacts to the body's natural movements, adding muscle power
to complement the user's strength (see page 032)

↑
The New Design for Old exhibition, held in the Boilerhouse Gallery at the V&A in 1986, put design for ageing on the map. The catalogue was designed by Lella and Massimo Vignelli.

In the 30 years between Helen Hamlyn's groundbreaking New Design for Old exhibition at the V&A's Boilerhouse and the Design Museum's decision to revisit the theme in 2017 at its new Kensington home, the worlds of ageing and design have both changed significantly.

Our understanding of what it means to grow older has broadened, with dynamic ideas around healthy and active ageing in a 'third age' of productive social engagement starting to replace a passive model of the 'elderly' confined to their own homes or institutional care. Similarly, horizons have expanded in design, with the rise of digital technology and other scientific advances. Standalone disciplines such as product or graphic design have been challenged and disrupted by the more integrated, cross-cutting approaches of service, interaction or experience design. Designers now work mainly in interdisciplinary teams rather than alone, and cultural exploration has become as important as technical resolution across all fields of design.

All of this might suggest an advantageous position for design and designers to respond to the needs of an ageing population in a creative way, and that is largely the case. But what hasn't changed in 30 years is the idea that demographic change is a ticking time bomb set to explode in our faces and that ageing is a burdensome thing. In fact, the faster we head towards an ageing society in which there are more old people than young, the more such thinking takes hold.

The NEW OLD project seeks to reverse that mindset, to give pause for thought with a simple message: design-led innovation can lighten the load of ageing. Through this approach, people facing greater longevity can enjoy fuller, healthier, more rewarding lives in the future – 'years full of life rather than life full of years'. This is not to ignore the medical realities of ageing – the physical, sensory and cognitive impairments that come to us all eventually. However, we must recognize that many older people are disabled by the design of the environment around them, rather than intrinsically disabled. Designers have a responsibility to use all the advances in practice and technology available to them to reimagine products, settings, systems and services that will enhance the experience of later life.

As curator of the NEW OLD exhibition, I set out to show both the dramatic scale of demographic change and the potential of design to frame an effective response to this challenge. The term 'new old' refers not just to the next generation entering later life – a cohort with quite different experiences and expectations from the 'old old' – but also the opportunity to think afresh about designing for an ageing society.

Two important markers shaped my curatorial approach. One was my participation in a two-year Foresight project led by Professor Sarah Harper of the University of Oxford to give recommendations to UK policymakers on the Future of an Ageing Population (Government Office of Science, 2016). My role was to lead on the environmental and infrastructure aspects of the research. It was a role that opened my eyes to the gap between need and provision for older people in the UK – in terms of housing, social connectivity, care, transport and much else besides – and the possibilities for new design to make a difference. The economic and social data shown in the exhibition and some of the essays in this book are drawn from the Future of an Ageing Population project.

The other significant marker was the New Design for Old exhibition from 1986. As Helen Hamlyn herself explains in this publication, leading individual designers of the day were commissioned to create new concepts to help older people to live independently in their own homes. We have revisited the idea of special design commissions with NEW OLD: projects by Yves Béhar/Fuseproject, Konstantin Grcic, Future Facility, Special Projects, IDEO and PriestmanGoode update the approach. Each commission forms the centrepiece of a different exhibition theme.

Reflecting recent shifts in design, these projects have largely been created by teams rather than individuals, and their focus on such themes as mobility, community, identity and work suggests a much broader canvas for age-related design interventions than the domestic environment. The design disciplines are broader too: the work on show is less object-based than it was 30 years ago – encompassing fashion, furniture, interior design, transport, service design, interaction design and experience design alongside robotics, material science and artificial intelligence (AI).

Indeed, the creative application of new technology to keep people healthier in later life is an underlying theme of NEW OLD, and a particular focus for exhibition co-sponsor AXA PPP healthcare. This has been extensively explored by the Design Museum through its alliance with the AXA PPP Health Tech & You Awards. It finds expression here through such work as Yves Béhar's Aura Power Suit, which demonstrates what is possible just around the corner, and IDEO's Spirit platform, an exercise in using AI to create community well-being 30 years in the future. Meanwhile, the Amazin Apartment concept created by Future Facility recasts the technology company as property developer, gathering data while providing stress- and maintenance-free accommodation for older people.

Living installation

Not all of the work in the exhibition is specifically high-tech. Konstantin Grcic's design to help older workers and thinkers engage with the outside world is inspired by a Renaissance painting; the 'living installation' conceived by Special Projects, so that exhibition visitors can converse with a real older person and write thoughts on paper, also leans towards the art world. And PriestmanGoode reinvents the micro-scooter. But it is undeniable that advances in technology are among the biggest changes of the past 30 years and will reinvent ageing over the next 30 years.

Emerging methods and techniques in a field known variously as 'inclusive', 'intergenerational' or 'universal' design will also exert a big influence, as governments and businesses around the world think about how to support more person-centred care with person-centred design. National initiatives from Norway and Japan are showcased in the exhibition and discussed in this book. The unexpected impact of New Design for Old led directly to the formation of the DesignAge programme and then the Helen Hamlyn Centre for Design at the Royal College of Art. Supported by the Helen Hamlyn Trust, the RCA has become a research pioneer in inclusive design. NEW OLD reflects this in its inclusion of several RCA graduates and spinout companies among the exhibits that flank the commissions in each section.

To coincide with NEW OLD, the Design Museum commissioned an exclusive survey from Ipsos Mori on attitudes to ageing in the UK. The survey, based on the opinions of more than 1,000 adults aged 16–75, revealed that a quarter of respondents would prefer to be cared for by robots in old age than by humans – and this rises to a third among young people. Clearly the next generation, influenced by the digital world, will have different ideas about what it means to be older – old age starts at 73 in the UK, according to the Ipsos Mori poll.

Deep-rooted stigma around ageing is often reinforced by youth-oriented media stereotypes. Working with Creative Review magazine, we also commissioned two advertising agencies to 'sell' ageing as desirable and democratic. Both Mother's elixir of age concept and Karmarama's campaign based on a library of wisdom containing dozens of titles all written by the same imaginary, mature writer, in their different ways, elevate the value of experience and challenge preconceptions about ageing.

As George Lee, co-founder of The Age of No Retirement and a driving force for intergenerational design, says in these pages, we need to counter a negative narrative around age. Design holds the key to achieve this. When we design well, we all become enabled – not disabled. Is anyone going to complain about technology that is too intuitive, customer services that are too helpful, packaging that is too easy to open, financial products that are too comprehensible, transportation that is too safe and comfortable, clothes that are too flattering or homes that meet lifetime needs? Of course not: inclusivity across generations is key.

Ageing populations represent one of the toughest global challenges we face. NEW OLD signals an end to the same old attitudes in design. I am grateful to the many individuals and organizations that have so enthusiastically and creatively contributed to the arguments advanced by the exhibition.

Jeremy Myerson is the Helen Hamlyn Professor of Design at the Royal College of Art and curator of the NEW OLD exhibition

NEW OLD
National survey on ageing
Ben Page

What will ageing be like for us? And what is 'old' anyway? When we asked the public on behalf of the Design Museum as part of the NEW OLD project, it became clear that being 'old' doesn't really start until you're 73 on average (and some eight per cent of us refuse to think of any age as 'old').

On average, the British expect to live to be 81, but many will live decades longer. In the UK today there are more than 500,000 people aged 90 or more, up from 185,000 in 1985. The number of people aged 100 and over living in the UK has risen by 65 per cent over the past decade – to 14,570 in 2015. These numbers will go on rising. One projection by the Office of National Statistics is that in 100 years' time, there will be more than one million people aged over 100 in Britain.

The key question, of course, is how we will live. Will we enjoy some autonomy and a good quality of life? Or will we be lonely, or managed in a rigid institutional setting? When we asked the public, the least popular place to live in old age is a residential care home – only one per cent prefer this option. Most want to live in their current home (31 per cent) or a new one by the sea or in a rural area (27 per cent). Another ten per cent want to live in their own home with adaptations.

It is clear that technology will become more important in old age. While most of us would like humans to help us wash and dress (76 per cent), a quarter of us would prefer robots (24 per cent), and among younger people this rises to a third.

What is going to help us most? The people we asked think driverless cars and sensors will be most helpful, but also welcome pretty much any technology that will let us keep our independence (see chart overleaf).

The challenge for designers will be to create low-cost, easy-to-use solutions that really make a difference. Most people are currently not saving enough to have a long, comfortable retirement, but there are other things we can all do. Our work for the Centre for Better Ageing has shown that while money and good health both matter in old age, the strength of your social network matters as much, if not more. So if you want a good old age, hang on to your friends!

Ben Page is Chief Executive Officer of Ipsos MORI

In October 2016, Ipsos MORI asked 1,100 people aged 16–75 in Britain to select from this list the three most helpful design innovations for older people in the future.

1   Exoskeleton suit to aid mobility (see page 032)

2   Robot assistant at home (see page 038)

3   Smart sensors in home environment for remote monitoring on a smartphone by your doctor and family

4   Serviced apartments with complete 'backstairs' control of appliances so that there is no housework (see page 074)

5   Clothes made from smart textiles for regular drug infusion

6   Artificial intelligence system that monitors your vital signs to manage diet and medication (see page 092)

7   Driverless vehicles to help you get around if you can't drive any more (see page 128)

8   None of these

9   Don't know

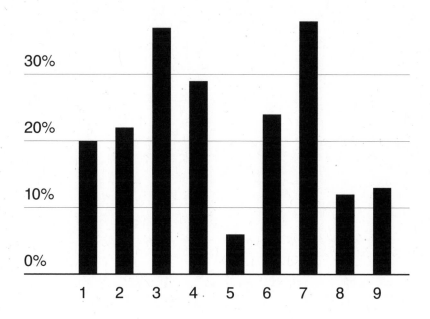

infographic
UK population estimates and projections in millions

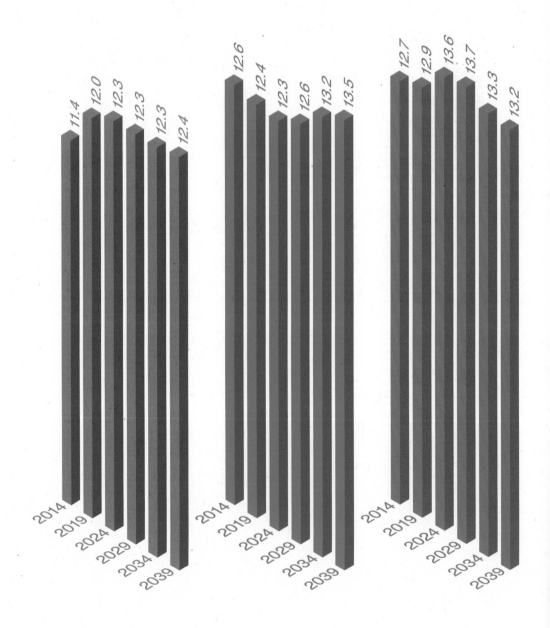

age	total population by year
0–14 years	2014: 64.6
15–29 years	2019: 66.9
30–44 years	2024: 69.0
45–59 years	2029: 71.0
60–74 years	2034: 72.7
75+ years	2039: 74.3

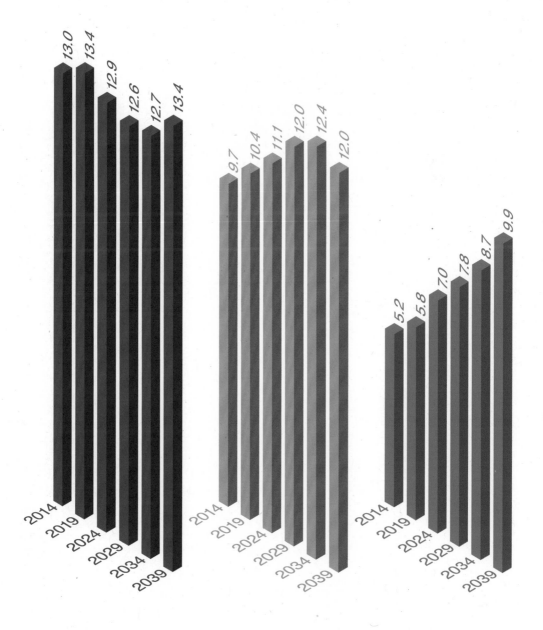

Throughout this book, each of these shapes is used to indicate an age group based on the number of its sides

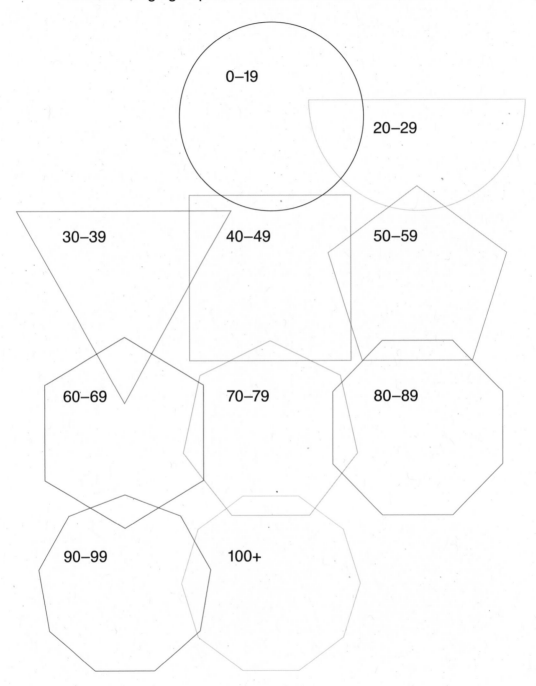

0–19

20–29

30–39

40–49

50–59

60–69

70–79

80–89

90–99

100+

NEW OLD
Ageing
Identity
Home
Community
Working
Mobility

'Having more older people
in society gives designers
a major innovation challenge.'

Like many developed countries around the world, Britain is ageing fast. It faces unprecedented change in the age structure of its population as the proportion of older people grows rapidly – the result of gradual increases in life expectancy and falling fertility and mortality rates.

In 2014, the average age of the UK population exceeded 40 for the first time – up from 33.9 in 1974. Seventy per cent of population growth in the UK over the next 25 years will be in the over-60 age group, which will increase from 14.9 million to 21.9 million people. By 2040, one in seven people in the UK is projected to be over 75 years old.

The presence of so many older people in society – living longer, working longer, travelling more, learning new things and requiring extended care – represents a major challenge for designers. Whether related to the built environment, technology or infrastructure, new design will be a major factor in how well we manage our ageing population. Governments and businesses alike will look to designers to create the innovations we need to tackle a demographic shift never seen before. But is design ready for ageing?

This is the question that the NEW OLD project asks. In this section, Professor Sarah Harper of the University of Oxford sets out the scale of demographic change, describing the UK as in 'a unique period in its history'. Harper identifies housing design as the most important element to get right. In response to a brief from the Design Museum to 'design a new product or service that is visionary and imaginative, doesn't currently exist and responds to the dramatic shift in age balance to the over-65s', designer Yves Béhar of Fuseproject presents two design proposals that cross traditional fashion and communication with advanced robotics.

'The afternoon knows what the morning never suspected.'
Robert Frost
Poet (1874–1963)

infographic
Perceptions of youth and old age across Europe

30s 40s 50s ▽ ▬ ⬠ youth ends   50s 60s ⬠ ⬡ old age begins

years of age

A European Social Survey of nearly 55,000 people aged
15+ showed varied perceptions of old age between countries.
In the UK, old age is perceived to begin at 59 – the second
youngest of the countries surveyed – and youth is perceived
to end at 35, again earlier than most countries.

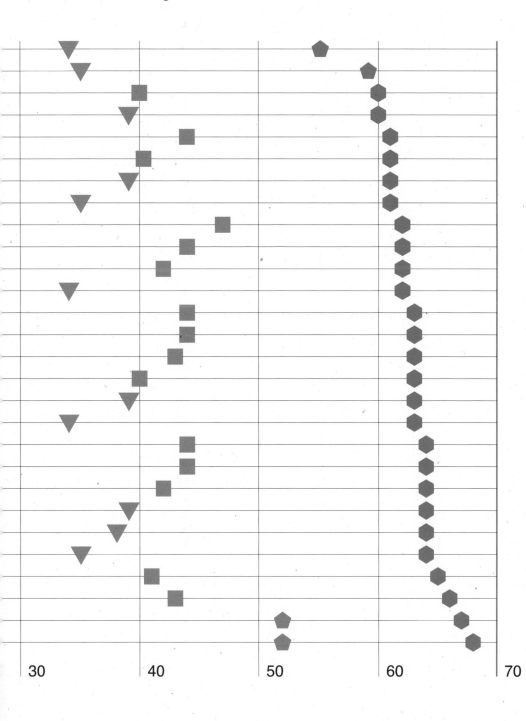

essay
Adapting to our ageing world
Sarah Harper

The twentieth century saw an ever-increasing number and proportion of older adults in many regions of the world – particularly in Europe. The European region became mature, with more people aged over 60 than under 16, over the turn of the millennium. There will be more old than young people in Asia by 2040, and by the middle of the century there will be more people over 60 than under 16 across the globe as a whole.

The UK thus finds itself in a unique period in its history. During the twentieth century, life expectancy gradually increased and the population slowly aged. With every year that passes, there is an increase in the proportion of people from successive birth cohorts who reach retirement age. Over the past 20 years in the UK, life expectancy at birth has increased by some five years – more than three months per year, or 15 minutes for every hour lived. As a result, old age is now extending.

Of particular note is the future life expectancy of our children – the number of those living past 100 years old will increase significantly. Indeed, it is now predicted that half of all children born in the UK will live to 103. This means that the number of centenarians in the UK is likely to increase from around 12,000 in 2016 to nearly half a million by the middle of the century and approaching 1.5 million by its end.

Some ten million of us currently alive in the UK (and some 130 million throughout Europe) are likely to live past the age of 100. In just over a decade's time, half of the UK population will be aged over 50. We have never had a society where half of the population is aged between 50 and 100 – quite simply, things have got to change.

In addition, the 'new old' will be different from the 'old old'. For example, those entering old age in 2025 will have had completely different life courses to those who are old now, and both will be different to those cohorts who become old from 2040 onwards.

Lifetime homes

This is where designing for our future selves becomes so important – and nowhere more so than our homes. Appropriately designed life-long homes are the future. We are all different, with varying needs and desires. While the older population is so diverse that it is inappropriate and undesirable to suggest an 'ideal' home, the home should enable people to maintain a good quality of life across their lives, and be adaptable to suit our changing family, work, education, health and care needs.

In the next 25 years, the proportion of UK households where the oldest person is 85 or over will grow faster than that of any other age group, and many more households will have at least one older person. With the growing widespread use of technology, our homes will become increasingly important for healthcare delivery, among other things. Smart home technology can enable remote monitoring, giving older people and their caregivers a greater degree of flexibility and choice. Other potential benefits include healthcare professionals advising patients about how to address problems at home, reducing the frequency of costly emergency visits and unnecessary hospitalization.

A reduced need for face-to-face contact for routine diagnosis and monitoring could potentially lessen the burden on our stretched healthcare services and allow healthcare to take place in a familiar environment where older people feel safe.

Making homes places for successful healthcare delivery will require greater attention to housing infrastructure, design and technological changes. Homes that meet the needs of older people, particularly for health and care, will be in great demand.

Homes may also increasingly become intergenerational living spaces. While we live in a society where independent living is prized, co-living may become more common with younger couples needing affordable housing and older generations nearby to offer and receive support as required. Good design and technology can help to create modern, flexible spaces that can be adapted for the eventual need for adult children to care for frail parents.

New world of work

Our world of work is changing fast. By 2030, the UK is forecast to have 12.5 million jobs, yet only 7.5 million people to fill those jobs. Across the 35 countries in the Organisation for Economic Co-operation and Development (OECD), there are more people leaving work than entering it, and in the UK we may no longer be able to rely on immigration to fill this gap. People aged 50–70 will need to contribute more and spend longer in the labour market.

In this new flexible world, homes will become increasingly important as places of work, both for younger and older adults. Older workers are already a fast growing group of home workers – able to combine economic activity with flexible leisure in the same space. Again, innovative infrastructure, design and technological changes will be needed to make our homes successful places of work.

Future housing has the potential to do far more than today's housing, and design will be at the centre of this. If we get the design of our homes right, we will make significant progress towards addressing the challenge of the UK's ever-ageing population.

Sarah Harper is Professor of Gerontology and Director of the Institute of Population Ageing at the University of Oxford

'We have never had a society
where half of the population is
aged between 50 and 100.'

The standard approach to designing for an ageing population has been to provide aid in the home to complete tasks and accommodate lack of mobility – which results in a life lived more statically. While these efforts to ease daily living activities are important, they fail to take on the greatest challenge for older people: mobility outside the home. Furthermore, the current framework for products in the design market – characterized by a clinical and 'sickroom' aesthetic – stigmatize ageing people and reinforce their increased marginalization from wider society.

All too often, lack of mobility due to muscle weakness, balance issues and coordination problems makes older people captive in their own homes. This has a cascade effect, increasing loneliness, isolation and depression (consider that more than half of women in the USA over 75 live alone). But what if technology could help us continue to move about the world and engage with it physically, socially and emotionally?

Our goal in designing for this exhibition is to show what technology can do for an ageing population right now. To do this, we partnered with Superflex, a commercial start-up that began in the Robotics Lab at SRI. Superflex is developing a new category of powered clothing – smart yet friendly, invisible, connected wearables that represent, in our view, the future of movement. Powered clothing aims to empower us by enhancing our physical ability so we can continue to live actively – bringing profound physical and emotional benefits.

With motors, sensors and AI embedded into a lightweight and flexible fabric, the Aura powered clothing provides support for the user's torso, hips and legs. It reacts to the body's natural movements, adding muscle power to complement the user's strength in getting up, sitting down or staying upright. In fact, powered clothing amplifies an individual's ability to move freely – actually improving muscle strength, balance and coordination. The Power Suit, including its embedded hardware, will weigh less than 1.4kg.

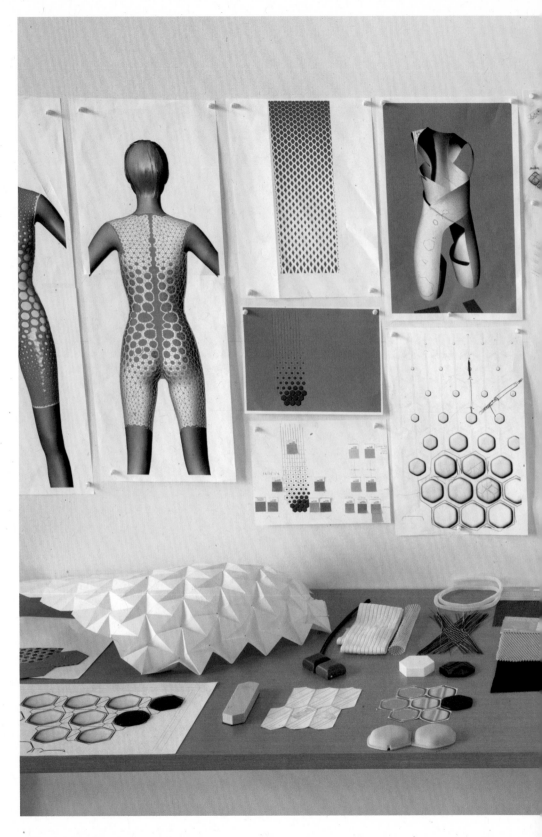

While most robotic technology and AI bring up dystopian notions, we have specifically designed the Power Suit to be easily adopted by, and useful to, older people. Using biomimicry, the suit configuration is anatomically aligned with the natural muscular composition of its wearer.

With maximum comfort in mind, the hard technology components such as motors, batteries and control boards are designed into hexagonal, low-profile cells. These cells are attached to fabric origami fold-ins that enable movement in three dimensions, allowing the hardware to expand, contract and move with the wearer. This supports a modular and scalable system that adapts to the muscular needs and heights of different users, with the ability to remove the hard cells to clean the garment.

Powered clothing has the clear ability to expand and extend our potential, providing people with the strength and confidence to participate fully and richly in the world. Expanding the social lives of an ageing population – extending the window during which they can remain independent, active and connected – is what Superflex and Fuseproject will enable in the immediate future. We are on the cusp of liberating a generation from a life of diminishing expectations.

←
Material innovation and design development of the Aura Power Suit

→
How the powered clothing provides muscular support

Applied Force

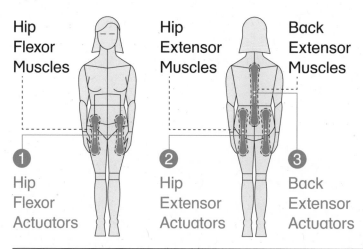

Hip
Flexor
Muscles

1 Hip
Flexor
Actuators

Hip
Extensor
Muscles

2 Hip
Extensor
Actuators

Back
Extensor
Muscles

3 Back
Extensor
Actuators

Power Assist

Core strength naturally declines as we age. The Power Suit augments your strength by aligning electric muscles with your natural muscles, actuating at the same time to assist your movement.

Age 75

Max Muscle Strength	Power Assist

Age 25

Max Muscle Strength

Sitting

•Torso support

Actuations in use:

Transition

•Torso support
•Gluteal augmentation
•Hip strength

Actuations in use:

Standing

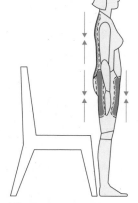

•Torso support
•Gluteal augmentation
•Hip strength

Actuations in use:

While it is important to stay physically active in old age, it's just as important to maintain a healthy level of mental and social activity. This will not only delay a plethora of diseases, but can also reduce loneliness – which 50 per cent of ageing adults list as their main concern. With this in mind, we worked with Intuition Robotics to develop an emotionally intelligent robotic companion, ElliQ, helping us to stay connected with loved ones, and to keep thinking and learning as we age.

Unlike our current perception of robots, this design is more akin to a beautiful table-top object, with a screen and 'character' structure designed to foster comfort and familiarity, eschewing the typical robot vernacular. There are infinite possibilities for defining interactions with this type of machine learning. Overleaf, we list the features most needed by the over-65s, according to our research.

Using natural language processing, with computer vision and emotion detection capabilities calibrated specifically for the needs of older adults, ElliQ interacts in the natural style of a companion, but with a unique aesthetic form that defines its own category.

With the screen and character distinct from each other, we were able to include a wide range of uses and expressions. The screen works on the cradle display, in the user's hand, or can stand on its own with an attached easel, showing video or other media content. The character structure uses diffused LED lighting to display expressions, with a wide range of motion for the 'head' to give it subtle personification in an accessible and friendly way.

Keeping these elements separate allows for broadened modular use, without breaking the emotional bond built over time with the character. ElliQ is a utopian example of AI for the near future – developing a relationship in which we can learn, grow and thrive as we age.

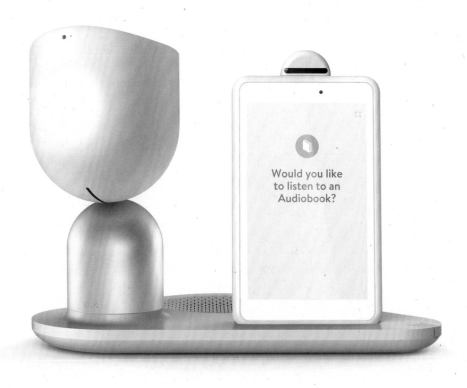

Coach

The design uses goal-based AI to learn the older adult's personal goals, like getting up more often, connecting with family or learning more on a particular topic. It then proactively nudges their activities toward these targets in a personalized manner.

Connector

The screen provides an easy way to video chat with family and friends and view the latest family photos, but the device is also able to send and receive text messages and calls or connect to social media.

Engager

The home companion can proactively suggest playing music, sharing news, finding and playing videos or reading audiobooks.

Companion

The structural character element can use speech, lighting, sound, images and movement to subtly convey emotion, showing understanding and support.

Lookout

The unit has a series of inbuilt monitoring features that can be turned on if desired, including the ability for a caregiver to check in with the device through social media.

Rendering of the intelligent companion, developed with Intuition Robotics

Elements of the ElliQ system

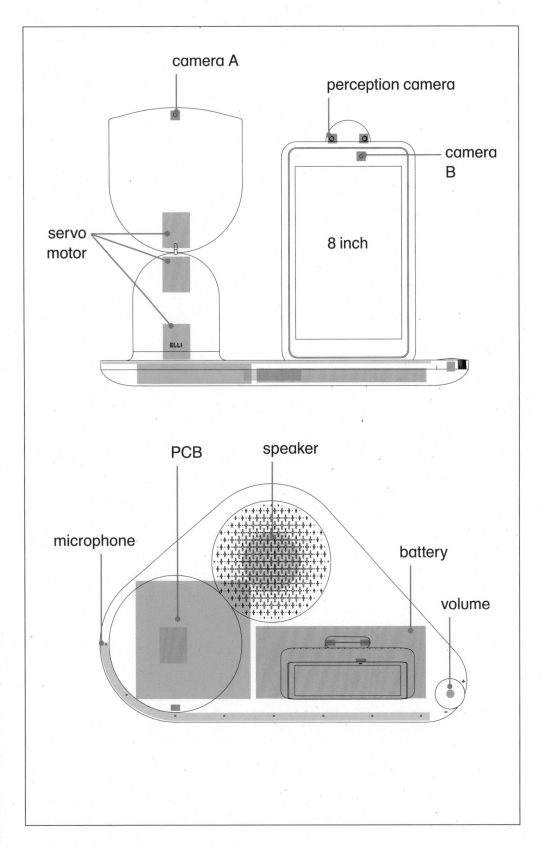

'Deep-rooted stereotypes around ageing endure... design can play a key role in removing stigma.'

Since the millennium, there have been more people over 60 in Europe than those under 16. But despite the steep rise in older adults in society, deep-rooted stereotypes around ageing endure. The stigma of growing old persists. Britain acknowledges this issue: in a social survey of some 55,000 people across 28 European countries, the UK was second only to France in recognizing that age discrimination is a 'very serious' or 'quite serious' problem.

However, the 'new old' of the next 30 years will be quite unlike the 'old old' of recent decades. The 'new old' will benefit from better healthcare, education and diet, and from changing social attitudes. This cohort will increasingly resist a medical model of ageing based on disease, decline and dependency, with new narratives related to active ageing.

Design and communication will have a pivotal role to play in the changing representations of older people in branding, advertising, the media and public discourse. In this section, George Lee and Jonathan Collie, co-founders of campaigning social enterprise The Age of No Retirement, explore how an intergenerational design approach might shift social attitudes.

In response to a brief from the Design Museum to 'design a new product, service, system or experience to tackle ageing stigma and cut down prejudice', designers Clara Gaggero Westaway and Adrian Westaway of Special Projects present a 'living installation'. This artwork gives exhibition visitors an opportunity to sit down and talk to a real older person, exchanging experiences and recording each conversation on a custom-built table comprising giant sheets of paper.

'I'm 63 and I guess that puts me in with the geriatrics, but if there were 15 months in every year, I'd only be 43.'
James Thurber
Humorist (1894–1961)

infographic
Perceptions of age discrimination across Europe

A 2010 European Social Survey study of nearly 55,000 people
aged 15+ indicated that respondents in the UK and France are
most concerned about age discrimination.

no discrimination

Belgium
Croatia
UK
Finland
Germany
Hungary
Czech Republic
Netherlands
France
Norway
Sweden
Slovenia
Poland
Greece
Slovakia
Romania
Switzerland
Israel
Portugal
Estonia
Bulgaria
Denmark
All
Latvia
Spain
Ukraine
Russia
Cyprus
Turkey

percentage of respondents   0%   10%   20%   30%

very/quite serious discrimination

Turkey	
Denmark	
Bulgaria	
Cyprus	
Russia	
Greece	
Croatia	
Ukraine	
Estonia	
Latvia	
Spain	
Slovenia	
Slovakia	
Belgium	
Switzerland	
All	
Germany	
Finland	
Czech Republic	
Sweden	
Poland	
Israel	
Hungary	
Netherlands	
Norway	
Portugal	
Romania	
UK	
France	

0%   10%   20%   30%   40%   50%   60%

essay
Shifting the negative narrative of age
George Lee and Jonathan Collie

The negative narrative of age is so powerful. The story that we hear, day in and day out, is of the looming 'demographic crisis' that is going to place a huge burden on our society as the population of older people grows. There are indeed challenges ahead, but there are also huge opportunities that come with an extended lifespan.

Ageism is still rooted in a society preoccupied by the seemingly arbitrary segmentation of the population along generational or age lines. According to Dara Smith, an attorney with the American Association of Retired Persons Foundation (AARP), 'We live in a society that normalizes ageism… making jokes about one's age remains acceptable, even as we've moved on from making similar comments about race, gender and sexual orientation.'

But society is changing. The linear life path – study, work, marry, have kids, retire, die – is over. College students could be 20, 30 or 60. First-time parents could be 20, 30, 40 and older. Moving into a new home can be a milestone for a new family, or for older empty-nesters who are downsizing. Grandparents could be 45 or 85. In this new world, people don't want to be treated like just another member of a demographic herd.

There are organizations that are seeing the new reality of the 'new old'. Todd Yellin, Vice President of Product Innovation at Netflix, typifies a new approach that goes beyond demographic segmentation in design and innovation. He explains, 'Everyone's instinct was that if you could find out people's age and gender, that's fantastic. But what we learned is that it is almost useless. What matters is not… gender, age or geography. It's not even what they tell you. It's what they do.'

But business leaders such as Yellin are still few and far between. The question that needs to be asked is, 'Are demographics still relevant?' Do we really become the same as everyone else up to 100 years old once we turn 50? Other labels – 'pensioner', 'retiree', 'baby boomer' – are meaningless, lumping individuals into narrow, homogenous groups. If we are going to make real impact, design and innovation has to be based around young and old alike, and what we have in common – because talk about difference just creates and perpetuates an unnecessary divide.

Age-neutral design

In the summer of 2016, The Age of No Retirement, a social enterprise at the forefront of changing the narrative on ageing and building a case for an age-neutral society, conducted a groundbreaking research project. We studied more than 2,000 people, ranging from 18–99 years of age, to explore general attitudes to 'age' in British society, and to ascertain whether an intergenerational approach to product and service design could be a powerful business driver as well as a societal game changer.

The findings shattered many of the age- and generation-related stereotypes that are deeply embedded in British culture, and indeed in the culture of many countries around the world.

The first key finding was that age does not define us – 83 per cent of respondents right across the age range felt like they are not like everyone else in their age group and that they want to mix with people from different ages and generations.

The research also got to the heart of challenging outdated but deep-rooted stereotypes around technology. It revealed that our aspirations in this area are aligned regardless of our age: 89 per cent of young people and 84 per cent of older people claimed that the Internet is totally part of their life, and both groups felt equally overwhelmed by the constant flow of new technology.

Nine out of ten respondents across the ages felt that there is too much age and generational stereotyping in advertising and the media. They felt that brands should focus on needs and interests rather than age, and eight out of ten respondents believed that age-neutral, inclusive brands are the most up-to-date.

One would expect that the more constrained cognitive, physical and sensory abilities of older people would make them more demanding consumers. But the research showed that the low tolerance of older people towards unnecessary effort in using products and services is more than matched by that of the young and middle-aged.

Retaking design

Overall, the research demonstrated categorically that our age is an increasingly misleading, limiting and stigmatizing construct. So how can we build on it? The answer is simple — by retaking design. To paraphrase the wise words of Pattie Moore, one of the pioneers of universal design (simply defined as designing products for as many people as reasonably possible), 'design can enable us or disable us'. Moore goes on to say that if we insist on categorizing people as either young or old, we create falsely conflicting camps for attention and action.

Universal design, or inclusive design as it is more commonly known in the UK, has been around since the 1990s. However, the seven core principles of universal design (originally developed by a research team at North Carolina State University in 1997) have not been updated since then, which largely ignores the entire Internet and mobile infotech industry that play such an important role in modern life.

The Age of No Retirement set out to update these seven principles in partnership with leading designers and researchers in the field of universal design. Ten principles of intergenerational design are shown opposite in draft form. They provide a blueprint for the design of all products, services and processes, across all sectors, to engage and serve a modern, multigenerational customer base.

All ten principles were tested among 2,000 people as part of the research project. While 86 per cent of people of all ages thought our intergenerational design principles were important, only 16 per cent thought that brands are applying them well. Age-inclusive design is the future of design. It is people-centric, not product-centric, and benefits everyone at any age. We just need to make it happen.

The 10 principles of intergenerational design

1 Safe and secure
Having your personal rights of safety, privacy and information security looked after and respected

2 Clear and intuitive
Being easy to understand and work out how to use

3 Free of time pressure
Optimizing your use of time, being neither too slow nor too fast

4 Delightful
Finding things to be pleasing, beautiful or enjoyable

5 Accessible
Being easy to find, reach or use either online or offline; being accessible as and when required, without being intrusive

6 Human connection
Helping you to feel connected to other people or have a two-way conversation

7 Flexibility
Being given choice, being easy to adapt and not punishing errors too harshly

8 Right effort
Needing the right level of physical or mental effort

9 Empowering
Feeling that things contribute to self and social worth, or that they help your development and autonomy

10 Sustainable
Finding things to be sustainable – socially, economically and environmentally

George Lee and **Jonathan Collie** are the co-founders of The Age of No Retirement, a social enterprise with a mission to create a world where age does not matter

The fashion industry has always promoted the glamour of youth. But many fashion brands today are seeking the glamour of ageing. From Joni Mitchell (in her 70s) as the face of Yves Saint Laurent and Joan Didion (in her 80s) as the face of Céline to the rise of Iris Apfel (above, in her 90s) as global style icon, fashion is tuning into older age.

project
No Country for Old Men
Lanzavecchia & Wai

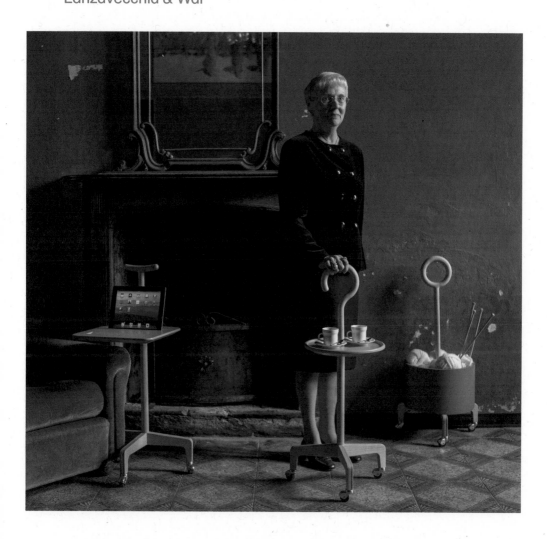

A collection of furniture that combines contemporary design with practical support for older people, challenging stereotypes around assistive living. The three Together Canes – the T-cane, the U-cane and the I-cane – enable traditional age-appropriate activities such as drinking tea, browsing magazines and knitting. It can also prop up an iPad.

Alan Dye of NB Studio teamed up with designer
Michael Wolff and Spring Chicken – a company that markets
age-friendly products – to create a campaign to change
the image of ageing. More than 70 designers submitted
alternatives to the UK's depressingly ageist 'elderly people'
road sign, ranging from the poetic to the absurd.

↑
Margaret Calvert
Marion Deuchars
Angus Hyland

↗
George Hardie

↗↗
Glen Tutssel
Purpose

→→
David Worthington
Oliviero Toscani

↘↘
Dave Anderson, Pocko
Harry Pearce, Pentagram

Tea junction

Slow down

The Design Museum worked with Creative Review magazine to brief leading advertising agencies to promote the benefits of ageing. Mother London's concept is to figuratively bottle the beauty of ageing (i.e. experience, perspective, wisdom) in an object of desire and place value on the years of our life through marketing tropes most commonly used in the world of fine wines and premium spirits – where age is a positive characteristic and translates as a sign of quality.

Creative Review advertising challenge
Learn from experience
Karmarama

Karmarama's approach to the Creative Review brief
to 'sell' ageing presents a bookcase containing dozens of
books all written by the same imaginary author, Sylvia Clark.
Sylvia is in later life, with years of experience behind her.
But she isn't a business guru, a politician or a sports star.
She is an ordinary person, expert in the ordinary stuff of life.
The title of each book addresses a specific subject, personal
to her but valuable to everyone. Together they represent the
ever-growing library of wisdom that we all carry around inside
us. The campaign encourages younger people to seek out
and make use of this wisdom – to learn from experience.

design commission
Exchange
Special Projects

Exchange is a living installation exploring ways in which
participatory design experiences can tackle ageing stereotypes
and stigma. The installation emulates the inviting, comforting
environment of a garden, with a large table and two chairs
at its centre, surrounded by greenery. It encourages members
of the public to engage in an informal conversation with an older
adult by sitting down with them and posing an open-ended,
personal question.

> What is the most valuable thing you have learned so far?
> What has made you the happiest in life?
> What is your biggest regret?
> How have you changed?
> Is it true that people don't grow up?

After responding, the older adult will similarly pose
a question to the exhibition visitor, together constructing a fleeting
game that sparks meaningful dialogue and an enriching exchange
of experience. All questions are recorded, creating a physical
artefact that catalogues exchanges between the installation's
changing protagonists.

The custom-built table and the entire top surface is made
from giant sheets of paper, stacked on top of each other like
the pages of an oversized notebook, encouraging participants
to write down their questions before asking them out loud. In this
way, the table also functions as an analogue bridge between
generations and a living archive that can be reviewed by other
exhibition visitors and used to spark new conversations.

This is an equal exchange, where no person is assumed
to be greater and wiser than another. The older adult learns
something from the younger visitor, and the visitor learns something
and perhaps challenges their perception of old age. By creating
a delightful and inclusive space for intimate cross-generation
conversation, Exchange urges us to expand our frame of reference
about what ageing is, and what it might become.

↑
An early model explored the green setting for the
Exchange installation

↑→
Crafting the setting in the Special Projects studio

'More adaptable and specialized
housing will be required in order
for older people to thrive.'

An ageing population in the UK will change demand for homes over the next 25 years, as more adaptable and specialized housing is required. The proportion of households including someone aged 85 or older will grow faster than any other age group over that period. Already, more than a third of households consist of older people living either alone or as a couple, occupying homes designed for families. Many of these people would like to move to a smaller home for health and family reasons but cannot find suitable properties. This puts additional strain on Britain's housing market.

In this section, architect and housing expert Judith Torrington of the University of Sheffield highlights the current mismatch between the UK's housing stock and people's needs in later life – and explores how design can help close this gap. In particular, she points out how 'cold, damp houses are dangerous for older people'. Future homes need to be safer and better insulated to reduce health costs. They also need to be adapted to support emerging work and care functions in the home, enabled by new technologies.

In response to a brief from the Design Museum to 'design a future-proofed home environment for independent living into old age', Sam Hecht and Kim Colin of Future Facility present a concept called Amazin Apartments. This explores the role of the technology company as property developer, providing the ultimate serviced apartment in which the older person enjoys anxiety-free use of built-in appliances and technology. The exhibition visitor sees both sides – inside the apartment itself and the hidden data-collecting service corridor that enables it.

'I have reached the age when,
if someone tells me to wear socks,
I don't have to.'
Albert Einstein
Physicist (1879–1955)

infographic
Reasons for moving home in England, by age

age
over 50s
over 65s
over 75s
over 85s

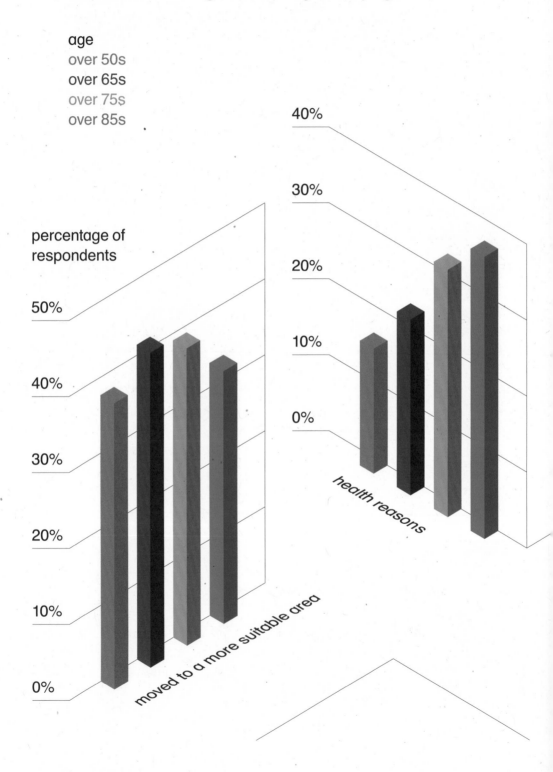

percentage of respondents

Reasons cited for moving home from 2004–2010 among more than 2,000 people aged 50+ revealed that the older people are, the more likely they are to move for health reasons or to be nearer to family members.

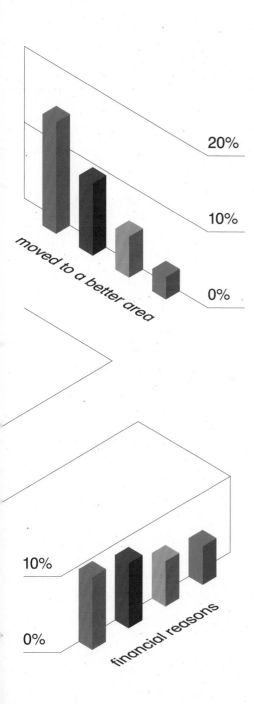

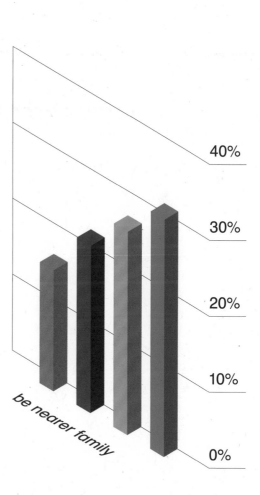

essay
Home design: is it fit for old age?
Judith Torrington

Nearly all older people live in standard housing in conventional neighbourhoods. In England, only seven per cent live in housing designed for older people or in residential care homes. Remaining at home, even in advanced old age, is a clear preference for most people – and why not? There is clear evidence of the benefits to well-being, autonomy and sense of self in living in a known and familiar setting.

On the face of it, this is a happy situation. But evidence suggests that UK housing stock is not well adapted to older people, and there are many mismatches between their needs and their homes. First, housing is designed predominantly for families – a typical home has three bedrooms and a garden. One consequence of increasing longevity is that, at a time of a significant UK housing shortage, a large number of older people occupy houses designed for bigger households.

There is evidence that older people would like to downsize but smaller, more easily managed homes are not available. Housing designed specifically for older people is available in diverse forms, offering varying levels of support, but it accommodates relatively small numbers across the country.

While specialist housing can be popular with its residents, it is a big step down for many people. Most sheltered housing apartments have only one bedroom, though more two bedroom ones are being built. Exchanging a family-sized home for one with fewer rooms involves jettisoning too much to make it an attractive option, so people tend to move into specialist accommodation only when their need for more support demands it.

How well does housing support the physical changes that accompany old age? People age differently but physical decline is inevitable: 45 per cent of the UK population over state pension age is disabled in some way. With age, nearly everyone experiences some loss of mobility and increasing difficulty in bending, stretching and weight bearing.

The key features of accessibility – level access, flush thresholds, wide doors and circulation space, and entrance level toilets – are found in only five per cent of homes in England.

Older people may have difficulty getting in and out of baths, walking upstairs, bending down and reaching up. Some of these needs can be met by adapting existing homes – fitting handrails, stair lifts, replacing bathrooms with wet rooms. But studies indicate that 16 per cent of homes would need major structural alteration to become fully accessible, and in 28 per cent of homes alteration would not be feasible.

Supporting health and well-being

Virtually everyone has some degree of sight loss as they grow older. NHS statistics indicate 64 per cent of registered blind people and 66 per cent of partially sighted people in the UK are aged 75 or over. Similarly, nearly two-thirds of people with hearing loss are 65 or older, and one in ten people in this age group have profound hearing loss. Homes are not designed to accommodate this sensory loss. Studies in the homes of people with low vision found that stairs and landings were not well lit – a matter of concern as the risk of falling downstairs is doubled for people with sight loss. Acoustic environments in local neighbourhoods, shops, restaurants and cafés are also often unhelpful to people with hearing loss.

Then there is the challenge of dementia. Estimates suggest there will be one million people with dementia in the UK by 2025. Many people with dementia live in care homes, but an estimated two-thirds live at home – around 560,000 people. Dementia is a life-changing condition for dementia patients and those who care for them. While each person's experience is different, managing dementia undoubtedly involves adapting the living environment. There is some excellent design guidance on design for dementia, but it is nearly all written with specialist accommodation in mind, rather than standard homes.

Large numbers of people with dementia and their carers could benefit from sensitive design solutions to the problems they face. People with dementia may turn gas cookers on and forget to light them, or leave pans to burn dry. Baths can overflow, and people can be scalded by hot water, pipes or radiators. It is often necessary to prevent people from walking away and getting lost, and find ways of keeping dangerous substances secure. At the same time, creating a sanctuary for a carer to relax and recharge can help to make a difficult role more bearable.

Neighbourhood design is also important for older people. Living in a supportive neighbourhood is beneficial to health, well-being and social connectivity, even if that neighbourhood is deprived. But accessing neighbourhoods can be difficult or impossible for older people if there are no step-free access points, ramps, handrails, seats or working toilets. Properly maintained surfaces and removing the seasonal hazards of autumn leaves and winter ice and snow are similarly essential to prevent older people from being confined to their homes.

There are also concerns about the condition of some housing, costing the NHS around £600m per year as a result of injuries alone. In 2012, 22 per cent of homes in England did not meet the 'decent homes' standard. Disproportionate numbers of older people inhabit housing in serious disrepair. Problems such as lack of insulation, damp penetration, poor heating, unsafe stairs and inadequate lighting affect people's health. And cold, damp houses are dangerous for older people, contributing to around 40,000 excessive winter deaths in England each year. Falls, particularly down stairs, are another major health risk for this group.

Potential for change

Most people in the UK can expect a long old age. Although physical decline is inevitable, this does not translate into misery – a 2016 Office for National Statistics survey found that 65–79 year-olds have the highest levels of personal well-being, though this declines in older age groups. There is potential for houses, furnishings and equipment to be much better fitted to the needs of an ageing population.

Currently, 24 per cent of the UK population is over 60, a figure that is expected to rise to 29 per cent in 2035. Large numbers of older people become invisible with advancing age, confined indoors by an unsupportive physical environment and/or physical disability. The aids and equipment that support old age are not generally found in normal shops; they come from suppliers specialising in disability, accessed via health professionals. In contrast, you can buy everything you need for a young child in supermarkets or on the high street.

The need for more and better-designed, age-appropriate housing in the public and private sectors has been recognized and supported across the political spectrum. Some exemplary new models have proved to be very popular with their residents and commercially successful, but they are not widespread. There is a wealth of design guidance and expertise available – the hope is that it can be taken on board.

Judith Torrington is an architect and formerly Researcher in Architecture at the University of Sheffield. She is the author of 'Future of Ageing: adapting homes and neighbourhoods' (Government Office for Science, 2015)

project
MiRO Dog
Sebastian Conran/Consequential Robotics

MiRO is a biomimetic robot companion designed
by Sebastian Conran in partnership with Consequential
Robotics, a spinoff company from Sheffield University.
Designed to be friendly and approachable but not toy-like,
MiRO interacts with sensors, wearables, a data hub and
assistive furniture as part of a total home robot system –
the Care Free Home System.

project
The Leaven Range
Simon Kinneir

Simon Kinneir has created a range of everyday kitchen products to give sensory feedback to people with sight loss. This jug facilitates filling and pouring to the right level through balance and touch. As you fill it up, the jug tips forward, providing feedback and giving the user more confidence.

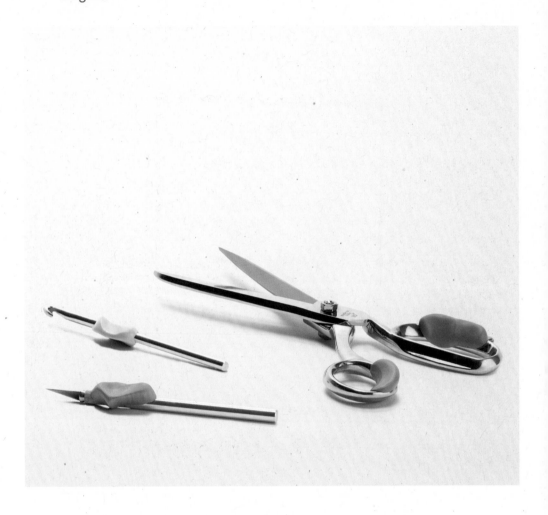

Small adaptations in the home can make a big difference
for older people. Sugru is a mouldable material that sticks
to almost anything. It turns into strong, flexible rubber,
enabling taps, switches or other items to be adapted
or gripped more easily. Invented by Jane Ní Dhulchaointigh
in 2003, Sugru is now used in more than 160 countries.

project
Beauty and ageing in the bathroom
Tomek Rygalik/Ideal Standard

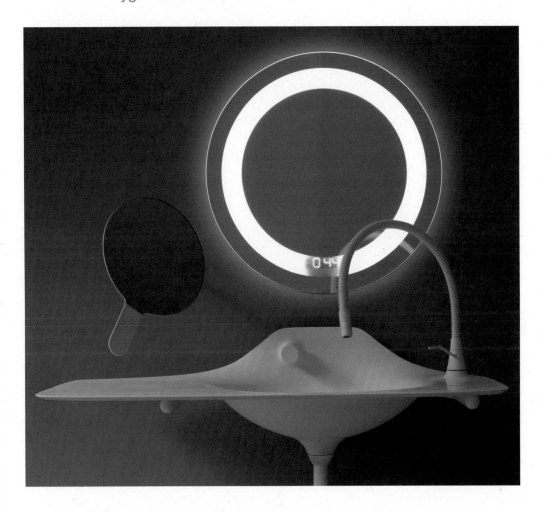

Bathrooms that include the needs of older people usually focus on safety and sterility. This Royal College of Art project, based on research conducted in the dressing rooms of older theatre performers, explores how the mirror and washbasin could create a sense of indulgence and luxury with a series of floating, glowing and flexible elements.

design commission
Amazin Apartments
Sam Hecht and Kim Colin, Future Facility

The following is paraphrased from a recent conversation with
my 87 year-old father. I arranged to replace his old tumble dryer with
a new one, to be delivered and installed in his flat by a reputable
national shop. With age, my father finds it increasingly difficult
to manage all the appliances and services required to maintain his
independence. He doesn't use the Internet. I thought I was helping.

Today

'Hi Dad, how are you?'

'The drier's packed up.'

'That's impossible – it's two weeks old! Have you spoken
to the shop?'

'They said I have to contact the manufacturer.'

'But you have a two-year warranty from the shop;
I made sure.'

'They said that if it breaks within the first year, I have to
go through the manufacturer – the shop won't deal with it.'

One week later

'Hi Dad, how's it going?'

'The drier's still not working. I couldn't get hold of the
manufacturer. When I did, they said they'd come in two weeks.
I'm fed up! A repair man from my local shop is coming this
week to fix it. I've got wet clothes here, piling up – I'd rather
pay and not wait another week.'

The next week

'Dad, how did it go with the repair man?'

'Well, he says it's broken. I'm fed up. He needs an expensive part to fix it and said I should get it replaced by the manufacturer because the machine's new and under warranty. That's £65 I wasted for him to tell me it's broken.'

The following week

'Hi Dad. How did you get on with the manufacturer?'

'They said it would be another two weeks before they could make the callout. So I got rid of that ****** machine. Got a new one from my local shop! Couldn't wait any longer. They installed a new one the next day.'

'What about the national shop – did they pick up the broken machine and give you a credit?'

'No, I got rid of it. Had to get it out of here for the new one to be put in. The local shop took it away when they installed the new one.'

Result

Paid twice for a new tumble dryer.
Paid for a service call from an independent repairman.
Got no refund or credit.

This conversation shows the difficulty that elderly people have in locating and arranging for products or services that they need for their continued independence. Despite the implicit promise of digital technology to make finding and buying things easier, there is a crisis afoot. Although services and goods are easily accessed online, they are less easily managed in the long term.

As we age, the world gets smaller and we increasingly rely on what we know, and what's local to us. We become less patient, less able to make decisions easily and less likely to wade through the conditions that shops and manufacturers require of everyday consumers. This puts the ageing population in a terrible position – abandoned at the precise time that they need increased assistance. Older people, alienated by the speed of change in trade, manufacture and technology, would benefit from a new way of maintaining independence. This is where Amazin Apartment comes in.

Tomorrow

The technology company becomes the property developer and manager. Imagine a more digitally savvy ageing population who will be fully able to use the Internet and harness all the services and products it offers. This population is already comfortable with ordering, banking, communicating, managing healthcare and other services online. So it is not a far stretch to imagine communities of people relinquishing the servicing and procurement of their domesticity to a technology company.

In fact, one could go as far as entrusting a company with maintaining appliances, delivering consumables, managing utilities and providing entertainment – all with our best interests and health in mind. It does not become a question of when something breaks, it is invisibly fixed even before you realize it is broken, without someone even entering your home.

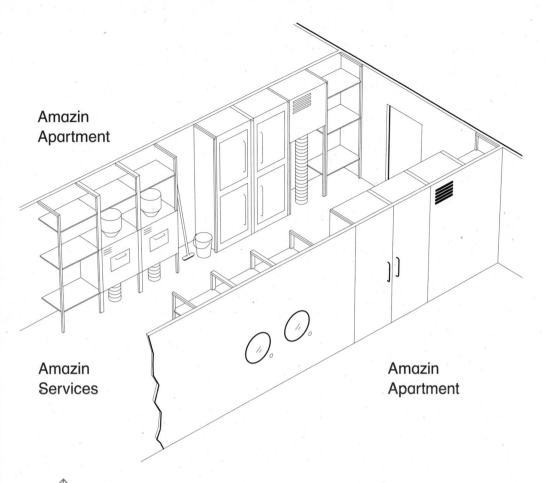

Amazin
Apartment

Amazin
Services

Amazin
Apartment

↑
Illustration of Amazin Apartment with Amazin Service by
Frederic Raetsch. The two sides of the wall are very different.

Technology companies feed off data. People in their final years might legitimately have enough of a cavalier attitude to allow a technology company to record, analyse and process their data without fear. When you are 80 years old, comfort, ease, care and peace of mind seem like fair exchanges for the data that you produce.

Amazin Apartment is a block where all apartments are serviced from an efficient network of unseen corridors, where appliances and technology are built into walls. These walls are serviced from the Amazin Service side by Amazin staff. Staff can replenish the refrigerator with fresh food, supply the washing machine with detergent, repair a dishwasher should it break, maintain the heating and air conditioning at optimum levels, all without entering the apartments.

Amazin staff receive and manage all goods and services as required, removing worries about maintenance and upkeep. Your experience with appliances is hugely simplified to their essential interface. The Amazin Service corridor, behind the apartment's walls, is organized like an advanced warehouse so that goods and services can pass through, be analyzed and replaced as needed with minimal impact on the apartment side. All appliances are designed to have two sides – the customer side and the service side.

This structure is not dissimilar to the way the Palace of Versailles or fictional Downton Abbey are arranged. The residents of these homes rarely saw the services or staff moving between rooms because of a network of service corridors and utility rooms hidden from the more formal public and private rooms. We conclude that the responsibility for quality of life among elderly people is too great to leave to appliance manufacturers. Instead, the new generation of technology companies, which have service as central to their existence (Amazon, Google and Tesla, for example), are in a far better position to deliver a more reliable and worry-free form of independent living.

↑→
Stills from the film Internet Machine that explores
data centres where Internet connectivity is managed.
The environment formed by this widely unseen service
network is the result of pure mechanical, digital and
functional requirements.

'Improved connectivity to ensure
that older people are not left isolated
will depend on better design.'

Successful ageing depends not just on designing better housing – how older people interact with the wider world in their neighbourhoods and communities is also critical to ageing well. Loneliness and social isolation can be exacerbated following retirement from work, the death of a partner, children moving away, ill health or reduced mobility. As a result, research suggests that a significant proportion of older people feel lonely some of the time or often, with those over 70 most likely to feel this way.

Connectivity between generations is therefore crucial in allowing people to interact socially and care for others. Designers can play a central role in developing the physical and digital infrastructures of connectivity – from neighbourhood design schemes and way-finding systems to virtual networks.

Other countries recognize the importance of a more coordinated and community-minded approach to design for older people. Japan is marshalling its industrial companies behind the needs of an ageing population through the International Association of Universal Design (IAUD). Norway has an ambitious government plan for universal design. In this section, Dr Yanki Lee reports on why a unique community of retired academics at Tsinghua University in China is ageing well on campus.

In response to a brief from the Design Museum to 'design a new community spirit that creates an intergenerational sense of belonging', IDEO presents Spirit, an artificial intelligence (AI) assistant for community wellness that is designed to strengthen social bonds 30 years in the future. To give a taste of an AI-boosted future, an interactive recognition system engages with exhibition visitors.

'Age does not protect you from love.
But love, to some extent, protects you from age.'
Jeanne Moreau
Actress (1928–)

infographic
Feeling lonely in the UK, by age and gender

A survey of 40,000 households in 2009–10 highlighted
the proportion of people who sometimes or often feel lonely.
Across all older age groups, women experience more
loneliness than men.

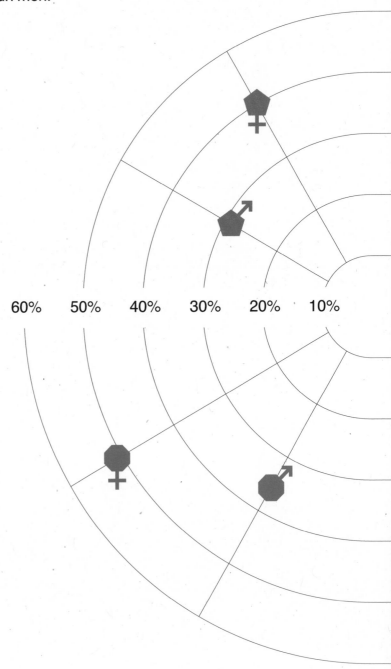

60%   50%   40%   30%   20%   10%

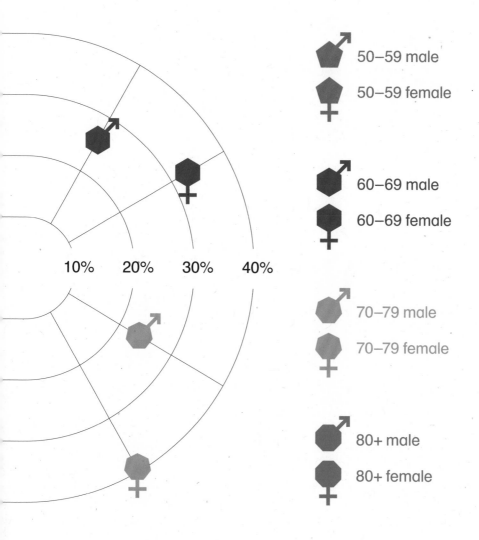

50–59 male

50–59 female

60–69 male

60–69 female

70–79 male

70–79 female

80+ male

80+ female

10%   20%   30%   40%

essay
The ingenuity of ageing well
Yanki Lee

Why do some people age well in their communities, while others do not? And how can designers respond to an unprecedented scale of demographic change that requires new approaches to community organization and engagement?

These are questions that have preoccupied me as a design researcher who looks at the social role of design. Indeed, they led to my involvement in an experimental piece of design research funded by the UK Government's Department of Business, Innovation and Skills. In 2012, I spent a year in Beijing on a UK-China Fellowship of Excellence programme, studying a remarkable community of 6,000 retired academics living on the campus of Tsinghua University.

The retirees on this campus are unique in the way they successfully resist the social definition and categorization of old age. Their lifestyle choices challenge the traditional model of older people as 'passive recipients' of product and services. In fact, they rely on their own ingenuity for social interaction and innovation. What could this novel community tell us about strategies for 'ageing well' in societies around the world?

I set out to investigate ways of engaging this group of ingenious older people and began designing specific interactions around the theme of five traditional Chinese festivals. With the support of design students, I created pop-up design stores to probe the retirees on living strategies. The stores were a useful place where we could invite the elders to co-design social innovation programmes for ageing populations on four main themes: health, leisure, knowledge and death.

Health innovations ranged from urban farming to new restaurant menus. Leisure looked at local travel groups as well as Internet and exercise clubs. Knowledge explored new ways to communicate and engage with younger people. And innovation around death spanned from greener burial methods to donating bodies for medical research.

As one of China's most renowned universities, Tsinghua is an important centre for nurturing talent and conducting scientific research. Its 6,000 retirees still live in the campus community alongside more than 30,000 students and 10,000 staff members. With pensions equal to half of their pre-retirement salaries and apartments for life, this group of retirees is financially free and independent.

Being, becoming and belonging

How well are individuals ageing within this collective? The Quality of Life (QOL) Profile defines our lives in three main domains: being (who one is), belonging (connections with one's environment), and becoming (achieving personal goals, hopes and aspirations). I adopted this profile as a framework to understand the health and well-being of these post-retirement individuals on the campus where they have been living with strong social networks for more than 40 years.

First, members of the Tsinghua retirement community have developed ways to maintain their individual physical, psychological and spiritual being. For example, they use their run-down apartment building (four- or five-storey blocks with no lifts) and take their old bicycles over rough terrain to maintain fitness; evidence suggests that using stairs and cycling has helped to keep their bodies flexible.

Second, they engage actively with their existing networks and even extend their connections with the wider community. One interesting case around the theme of belonging is that of a trained chemist who decided to research oxygenation after retirement with the support of younger colleagues, due to his own health and using his own body for tests. This led to a national patent for an invention called Fitness Oxygen.

Finally, in the becoming domain, I observed members of the Tsinghua community articulating the ageing experience as knowledge to help others to age well. An architectural professor joined our project and edited two books of stories about ingenious older people from other countries. He gradually became an advocate of productive ageing and a campaigner for job opportunities for retired people.

Cultural model of ageing

Gradually, a picture emerged of a group of innovative people working and stimulating each other to tackle persistent myths about older people and a culturally based fear of ageing. It became clear that their unique situation of collective living has become an incubator for social innovation, with co-design and participatory design processes enabling greater individual choice and control.

Through the lens of ageing and ingenuity, we gathered evidence on many important topics around ageing – from cognitive impairments to coping strategies for chronic diseases. This information helps to identify which new services, tools and solutions will best serve a future ageing society.

Based on the Tsinghua experience, ageing well within a community does not conform to a medical model of ageing as a disease to be cured by experts. Neither does it conform entirely to the social model of ageing, even though social connectivity with others is recognized as important. By focusing on design as a citizen's right and making every aspect of daily life an holistic celebration of autonomy, Tsinghua exemplifies what I call the 'cultural model of ageing', in which boundaries are moved and new perspectives for change are opened up.

Dr Yanki Lee is co-founder of Enable Foundation, a social design agency based in Hong Kong. She is also Director of DESIS Lab for Social Design Research at the Hong Kong Design Institute and the author of 'The Ingenuity of Ageing for Designing Social Innovation' (UK Department of Business, Innovation and Skills, 2012).

'A cultural model moves beyond
the medical view of ageing as
a disease to be cured.'

project
Staiths South Bank, Gateshead
Hemingway Design

This 760-home development on the banks of River Tyne
was designed with architects Ian Darby Partnership
and built by Taylor Wimpey. It embraces community values
in a contemporary setting and rethinks affordable housing
design. No two homes are identical. Private gardens open
onto shared green spaces with communal facilities such
as barbecues and table-tennis tables for intergenerational
exchange.

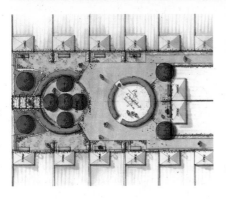
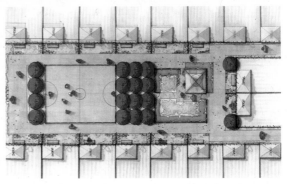

design commission
Spirit
IDEO

How did you decide who you are spending your life with: your partner, friends and colleagues? If you are like most people, you probably trusted your gut. But as everyone who has broken up with a lover, let a friendship fade or quit a job because of their boss knows, our stomach sometimes leads us astray.

We frown at the idea of objectively evaluating a husband, friend or work buddy, but these incredibly complex decisions are among the most important we ever make. These people – our community – are literally life-saving as we get older. Facing physical infirmity, far-away family members and retired from work, our social bonds are liable to unravel, particularly if we weren't well-matched in the first place.

Philosopher Alain de Botton argues that the reason we sometimes make poor decisions about people is because we don not understand ourselves, and certainly not others. But what if you did? What if you had a sixth sense that meant you knew who to marry, who to be friends with and who to work with, that guaranteed a close-knit network into old age? What would you give – or, perhaps, give up – for that?

Meet Spirit: your social assistant
As a visitor to our exhibit, you can ask that question – literally. We've created an interactive installation introducing Spirit, an artificially intelligent assistant designed to strengthen your social bonds.

Spirit is like Apple's Siri, Microsoft's Cortana or Amazon's Alexa but imagined for the technologies we expect to see 30 years from now. We show you the everyday social life of a Spirit user, Simon, and explain how AI augments his personal network. And to give you a taste of an AI-boosted future, we've built a face- and emotion-recognition system that interacts with exhibition visitors.

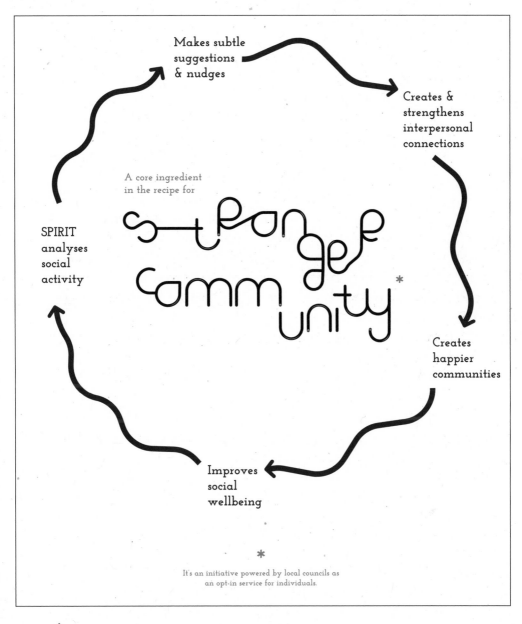

Makes subtle suggestions & nudges

Creates & strengthens interpersonal connections

A core ingredient in the recipe for

STRONGER COMMUNITY*

SPIRIT analyses social activity

Creates happier communities

Improves social wellbeing

*

It's an initiative powered by local councils as an opt-in service for individuals.

↑
Community builder: diagram exploring the social benefits of the 'Spirit' assistant

How will Spirit work in the future? Instead of just sharing our emails, web searches, location and photos with Apple, Google and Facebook (as we do today), we envisage a world where we will give Spirit permission to access who we speak to online and in the real world, the books we read and the films we watch. But also – through biosensors in our bloodstream – what we eat and drink. Sensors will travel into our brain, capturing our every physical, emotional and psychological response to people, places and things.

Spirit's AI will build a fine-grained profile of you and how people affect you. In short, it will discern how our friends, family and colleagues keep us socially connected, mentally stimulated and physically active as we get older.

A digital adviser

But how might Spirit share that information with you? The merging of biology, design and technology will mean your body itself will be an interface.

Spirit will proactively manage your calendar. And when you are with a friend, tiny nanobots clustered around your cheeks and jaw will vibrate, whispering helpfully in your ear to enhance your conversations. What might it say? Perhaps a recap of your last meeting, or recalling the vintage brooch your daughter liked before her birthday, or even the name of a former colleague's football team to ease an awkward conversation.

Body language

Beyond making you a better conversationalist, Spirit will help you meet people who would be good for you. By constantly comparing your profile to other (consenting) Spirit users, it can predict a great friend, co-worker or student, and physically nudge you to let you know.

When we love someone, we feel butterflies in our stomach. When we are frightened, our hackles rise. When we are lonely, we feel heartache. But these primordial cues are opaque and not always helpful. What if your instincts could objectively be right? What if they could act in your physical, mental and emotional best interests, supercharged by powerfully accurate AI?

Spirit will do that: it will speak to you through a new language of artificial bodily sensations, triggered by nanobots nestled in your brain, muscles, skeleton and organs. A tingle down the spine might alert you to a student you would benefit from teaching. A bad taste in the mouth might indicate that you are speaking to someone you would not get along with.

Over time, Spirit's helpful whispers and subtle physical sensations will help build a strong, healthy community around you, perfectly calibrated to your personality, temperament and emotional needs – and you, in turn, matched to their needs.

The oracle of data?

Would we in time come to trust Spirit's artificial senses more than our own? As creepy as that thought might be, it is worth reflecting how algorithms guide our lives. Who we date, the news we read, the friends we hear from, the books recommended to us are shaped by OKCupid, Facebook, Google, Amazon and others.

As we use these online services, we give them data to improve and we trust them more. Perhaps that's OK when we're deciding between watching Game of Thrones or Mad Men. But as that trust improves, we might begin to ask questions we once thought only humans should answer – what career to pursue, who to befriend and perhaps, even, who to marry.

Knowledge, power and responsibility

As human-centred designers, creating Spirit has made us think deeply about the increasingly influential role that technology plays in our lives. Biosensors, nanotechnology and AI might seem like science fiction. But today's emerging technologies are tomorrow's design tools. As our lives and societies are shaped by these technologies, how we design services such as Spirit becomes hugely significant.

So it is more important than ever to place human agency at the heart of what we design – that we augment, rather than automate away, the richness of human experience.

'A new design approach
can enhance the productivity
of older workers.'

As the population ages, our working lives will extend and fewer people will retire in their mid-60s as in the past. The importance of retaining older workers is also set to grow as employers face a gap in the labour market. Research suggests that 12.5 million jobs in the UK will be opened up by 2020 through people leaving the workforce but there will be only seven million new workers to fill them. Longer working lives will not only plug skill gaps and reduce welfare bills, but can also bring health and cognitive benefits if work tasks, work tools and workplaces are designed more appropriately for older people.

Design changes are required across multiple employment sectors, including white-collar workplaces, construction and manufacturing. In this section, Professor Peter Buckle of Imperial College London calls for a more holistic approach to designing workplaces for an older workforce, to enhance productivity and counter negative attitudes to age.

In response to a brief from the Design Museum to 'design a product, service, system or experience that helps people want to work for longer', Konstantin Grcic presents an outdoor structure for working and thinking. This metal structure is open to the sky, with a form that challenges an outdated image of older people related to disability. It is inspired by Antonello da Messina's fifteenth-century painting 'Saint Jerome in his Study', a famous portrait of a person of advanced years completely absorbed in their work.

'Anyone who stops learning is old, whether at 20 or 80.
Anyone who keeps learning stays young.'
Henry Ford
Founder of Ford Motor Company (1863–1947)

infographic
Employment rates of older people in OECD countries, by age

55–59
60–64
65–69

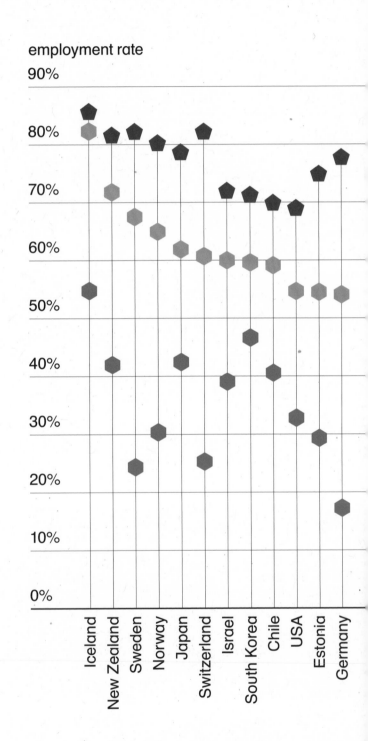

employment rate

In 2015, Britain's employment rates for older people were around the average for OECD countries. If they had been as high as those in Sweden between 2003 and 2013, UK national GDP would have been £100 billion higher.

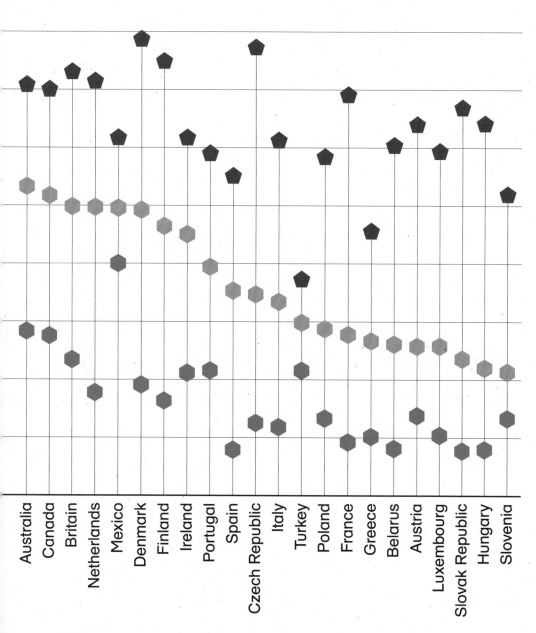

essay
Supporting an ageing workforce
Peter Buckle

Today's workplaces must accommodate an ever-widening demographic age range. This necessity arises from generational longevity and the increasing burden this places on pensions and related welfare benefits. Retaining older workers with specific skills and know-how is likely to be increasingly important to employers as people face longer working lives.

But what workplace and environmental infrastructure changes may enable a larger number of people to remain successful and productive in the workforce beyond traditional retirement ages? And what is the potential for supporting people to remain in employment while also enduring common health ailments that affect an older population?

I recently reviewed significant literature in this area as part of the UK Government's Foresight Future of an Ageing Population project, which set out to explore the policy and practical adaptations needed to respond to such a profound demographic shift. This essay sets out key findings from my review.

At the outset, I recognized that defining the workplace infrastructure requires an understanding that each element in a work system may interact with others. These interactions affect the performance, behaviour and well-being of those working within it. So, to consider any one element in isolation is unlikely to be appropriate.

The elements that must be considered include the use of physical devices, use of ICT, the design of the physical workplace and 'softer' elements such as team and group behaviour, work organization and management. Interactions between these components are ubiquitous and central to ergonomics, the discipline used to construct my review.

I identified a number of key issues through the review. First, the demographic modelling of the future workforce is generally poor. Until this is addressed, assessing the needs of older workers and prioritizing resources and design needs will remain largely speculative.

Second, while older workers are considered valuable employees because of their knowledge, skills and experience, managing an ageing workforce requires additional training to maximize their motivation, potential and contribution. Programmes to enable managers to achieve this are available in some European countries, notably Finland, but appear to be largely lacking in the UK.

Third, the physical and psychological work demands on older workers frequently exacerbate existing health conditions or lead to ill health. Improved design of work systems, including equipment and the organization of work, should make use of the extensive knowledge base on the needs and capacities of older workers.

Finally, designing work systems (including technology) for older workers requires co-design or participatory approaches that properly engage that cohort. It is evident that work system interventions based on one workplace factor alone are unlikely to demonstrate a significant effect. This is because work is a complex system in which many elements are interrelated.

Sector-specific policy is needed as requirements vary greatly across industrial work sectors. This is particularly noticeable where technology is advancing rapidly or where physical work demands remain high, such as construction or manufacturing. Evaluation of the impact and benefits of workplace interventions and designs, based on well-designed trials, is urgently needed.

Office work

When one looks at knowledge workers in offices, there is considerable guidance on how workspaces might be designed for an ageing workforce to accommodate changes in vision, hearing, physical ergonomics, cognition, and general health and well-being. However, there is an extremely limited evidence base assessing the impact of these interventions.

A lot hinges on the need for a more flexible and adaptive workspace to meet the needs of an ageing workforce. In particular, there is a need for office areas where tasks requiring analytical skills and concentration (the solo aspect of knowledge work) can be undertaken, as well as spaces for contemplation and recuperation.

The cumulative evidence suggests that traditional open-plan offices are less good for employee health. Given the needs of older workers, this may have a more pronounced effect on their performance and well-being than that of younger workers. This may be because working in open workplaces increases cognitive workload and worsens interpersonal relations.

Construction

In construction, around a quarter of the workforce is aged over 50, representing at least 600,000 workers, according to a 2013 study by the UK Government's Department for Work and Pensions. Research in this sector suggests that both physical job demands and psychosocial job characteristics (such as preventing emotional exhaustion) play a significant role in people's ability and willingness to continue working until the age of 65.

Older workers are more exposed to overload than their younger colleagues because their physiological capacity and muscle strength is generally lower. Boosting fitness in this group can be seen as one ameliorative measure. Providing adequate opportunities to do this might be part of a broader approach that might include encouraging older workers to join a gym, cycle or walk to work, or eat more healthily.

Another strategy is for construction workers to transition from harsher, fast-paced industrial work to 'slower' maintenance work in an attempt to reduce health problems. Guidance for employers on how best to manage an ageing construction workforce has emphasized the use of a participatory design (co-design) approach to enhance the workplace environment and equipment. Such an approach has the added advantage of potentially improving the quality of working life for both younger and older workers.

Manufacturing

In the manufacturing sector, research suggests that general physical changes in the older workforce could be offset by increased mechanization and automation. There is, however, a potential trade-off in such scenarios. An increase in mechanization and automation may place higher cognitive and other psychological demands on the workforce, for example isolation.

The literature surrounding cognitive changes associated with ageing is harder to interpret as there is much individual variation and the changes may be subtle. Perceived 'workability' may be important in this regard, and some organizations and manufacturing plants have started to address this challenge. For example, BMW has introduced an initiative to create a more age-diverse workforce in its car-making plants, entitled Today for Tomorrow.

BMW's approach has included implementing more than 70 small changes that improve the efficiency of an experimental production line (incorporating, for example, magnifying glasses, stretching stations, wooden floors to improve cushioning and insulation, and ergonomically designed standing chairs). Many of these changes are a result of employee input using a co-design approach, playing to older workers' strengths in terms of patience and skill.

In conclusion, the design principles required to improve workplace infrastructure, as described in the sectors above, must cover the need to make and test adjustments. This includes the physical work environment, the psychosocial work environment, workers' skills, work organization and age management.

This review has demonstrated the connectivity between these factors. It seems likely that these must all be addressed simultaneously through a participatory design approach. Paying attention to the physical infrastructure or technology infrastructure alone will not be sufficient for our ageing workforce.

Professor Peter Buckle is Principal Research Fellow in Human Factors in the Department of Surgery and Cancer, Imperial College London, and the author of 'Workplace Infrastructure' (Government Office for Science 2015)

project
Sky Planter
Boskke

As employers respond to the need for healthier working across the generations, the ingenious ceramic Sky Planter brings biophilia to urban offices where floorspace is a precious commodity. Developed by brothers Jake and Patrick Morris, Boskke uses its own Slo-Flo irrigation system to provide each plant with water for up to two weeks at a time.

BMW Group has pioneered a range of design and ergonomic initiatives on its production line in Dingolfing, Germany, to address the needs of an ageing workforce. It is now rolling these out internationally. Here, an employee sits at a height adjustable seat on a cushioned floor and a 'pick by light' system shows the part he needs next.

This project, in partnership with Samsung, explored why
older people can be reluctant to use smartphones. A key
problem identified by the research was setting up the phone.
The designers created a manual in the form of a storybook
that contains the phone and releases it to the user as they
turn the pages and follow the graphic instructions for set-up.

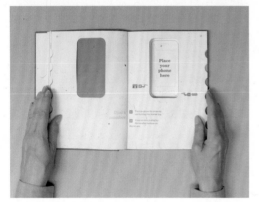

Place
your
phone
here

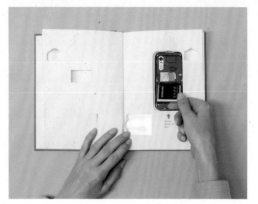

HEAD IN THE SKY is an outdoor space for working and thinking.
It is a safe concentration place for people of older age, who
are still living life to the full and do not want to retreat into their
own private domain, especially mentally. The title hints at the
opportunity to keep a clear head with advancing age, to dream
and imagine.

While the object is open at the top to give thoughts free
rein, verticals along the sides constrain the space. The notion of
envelopment and enclosure, inspired by Antonello da Messina's
painting 'Saint Jerome in his Study' from 1475, was developed
further for working outdoors. The zinc galvanized-mesh structure
offers an opportunity for seating, a form of table and the hint
of a shelf within a limited area. The weatherproof material screens,
yet remains permeable.

The construction is loaded with meaning with respect to
the topic 'new old': the long ramp signalling wheelchair access
formally makes a clear reference to an outdated image of old
people. For me, it symbolizes departure and a new beginning.

↑
Konstantin Grcic's mesh structure for outdoor
working connects working workers to the country
rural landscape outside

↑
Saint Jerome in His Study, Antonello de Messina's painting
that inspired Grcic's structure

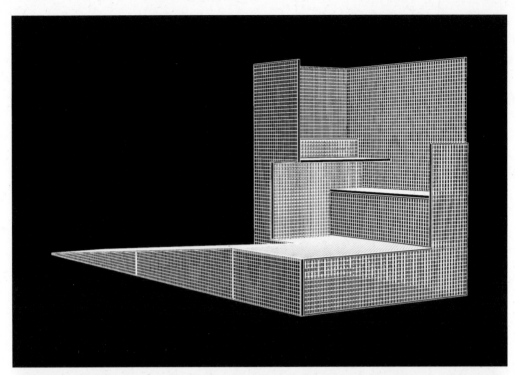

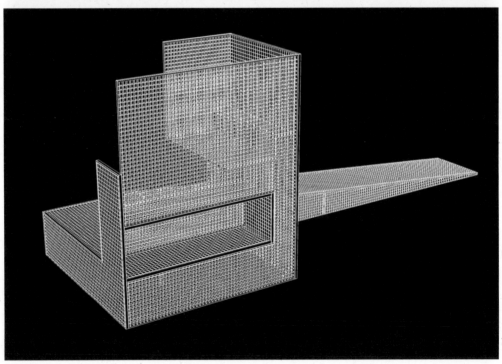

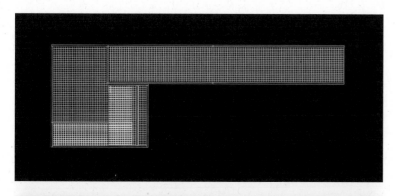

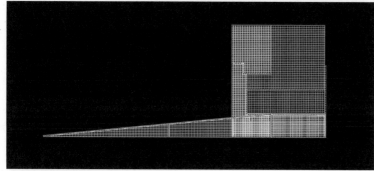

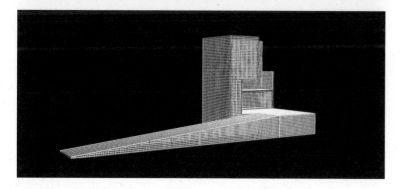

'Designers must address the
many barriers to mobility that
affect the health of older people.'

Maintaining mobility is vital for an ageing population. Loss of mobility has a direct impact on health and well-being. Being able to get around is important for practical reasons such as working or shopping but also for social connection, identity and self-esteem. Although people aged 50–59 travel more than other age groups, those aged 70 and over travel significantly less, covering only 64 per cent of the average distance travelled across all ages.

Retirement to rural areas with poor public transport exacerbates mobility problems for older people without access to a car. Public spaces in cities that lack social amenities such as seating, toilets and step-free access put up further barriers to mobility for older people.

Designers will be increasingly busy creating new mobility solutions for the 'new old'. From electric bicycles and folding wheelchair wheels to fully autonomous vehicles, technology and engineering is setting the course. In this section, Rama Gheerawo and Professor Dale Harrow of the Royal College of Art look at the past, present and future of driverless cars, and how they might affect the all-important last kilometre of any journey made by older people. Might autonomous vehicles even help bridge the gap between different generations?

In response to a brief from the Design Museum to 'design a future product, service or system that keeps people on the move as they get progressively older', PriestmanGoode has designed a Scooter for Life that can be adapted over time as our mobility requirements evolve, offering older users greater independence without the stigma associated with a mobility scooter.

> 'You know you're getting old when all the names in your black book have MD after them.'
> **Harrison Ford**
> Actor (1942–)

infographic
Travel in England by age and purpose

50s 60s 70+ purpose of travel
                commuting/business
                shopping
                visiting friends
                holiday
                other

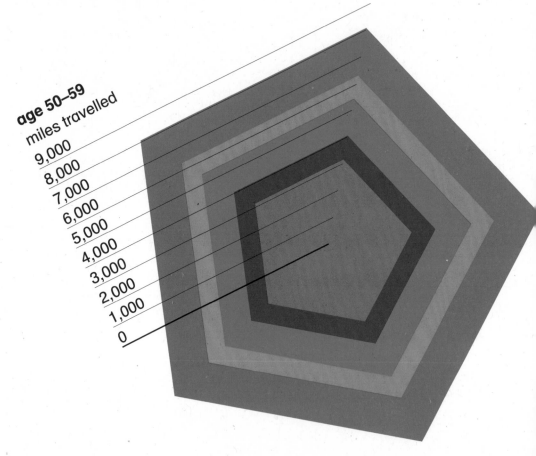

age 50–59
miles travelled
9,000
8,000
7,000
6,000
5,000
4,000
3,000
2,000
1,000
0

This graphic shows the miles travelled per person per year in England in 2014, based on a survey of 17,000 people. It illustrates how horizons shrink as we age, particularly for those over 70.

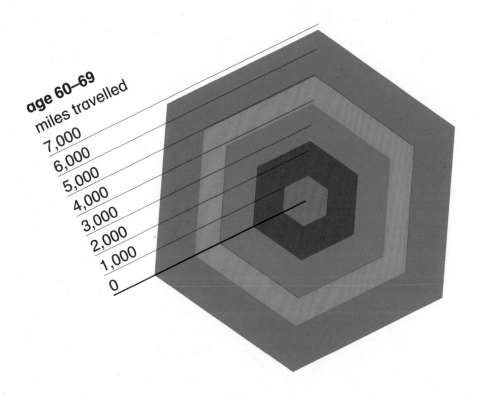

age 60–69
miles travelled
7,000
6,000
5,000
4,000
3,000
2,000
1,000
0

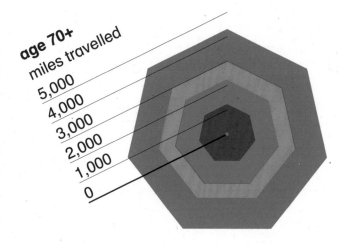

age 70+
miles travelled
5,000
4,000
3,000
2,000
1,000
0

Driverless cars in the age of ageing
Rama Gheerawo and Dale Harrow

From folk tales of flying carpets to appearances in science-fiction movies, autonomous vehicles have gripped our imagination around the world. Now, mobility is set for the greatest change since the invention of the internal combustion engine. People see the rise of driverless cars in a variety of ways, from the excitement of new possibilities and eagerness to try them to fears over lack of control and outright scepticism.

Driverless vehicles could bring real benefits for older people, through maintaining mobility and accessing community services. Mobility is a key indicator of quality of life, with ownership of a driving licence still important to many people. Losing their licence because of health or sensory decline can significantly affect people's self-worth.

Easy-to-use driverless cars could allow everyone to drive, regardless of age or ability. A visual impairment or significant loss of dexterity would not be a barrier to using a vehicle, creating radical new possibilities for more inclusive mobility.

The last kilometre of any journey can pose significant issues for older people who find walking long distances challenging. Existing modes of public transport such as trains, buses and trams typically get people fairly close to their home, leaving taxis or private cars as the only true forms of door-to-door transport. A driverless car could become part of a truly door-to-door transport network. This is particularly valuable in suburban and rural contexts where public transport services tend to be less regular and further from people's homes.

Although driverless cars can feel futuristic, vehicle autonomy has been around in different forms for a while. Late nineteenth-century and early twentieth-century horse-drawn milk floats in the UK often relied on the horse to stop in front of each dwelling to allow the milkman to make deliveries. In countries where horses and carts are still prevalent, stories abound of the animal finding their way home if the driver was incapacitated.

Auto-helm systems have been used on boats since the nineteenth century, with electronic systems now optimizing many journeys without human input. Many of us step on a plane with little realization that an autopilot system will do most of the flying, especially the complicated bits such as landing. In fact, international aviation standards mandate that planes with 20 or more seats need to have some form of autopilot and modern jetliners often self-correct more quickly and accurately than a human.

Autonomous trains are perhaps the closest contact that most of us have had with a driverless experience. London's Victoria Station was the first to have automatic train operation in 1967. Various levels of automation have appeared since, from those supported by a person to fully automated systems such as Gatwick Airport's People Mover that launched in 1983. The positive public perception of trains may go some way to help reduce anxieties and fears around driverless cars.

On the cusp of change

Today, we are on the cusp of a significant change as autonomous vehicles approach everyday travel. The development of autonomy, electrification and connectivity are driving change – with potentially huge benefits in terms of safety, traffic congestion and convenience, which will smooth adoption.

The motor car, the defining machine of the twentieth century and the technological achievement that facilitated private transport for the masses, is the basis for the driverless car of the twenty-first century. The birth of modern car design was dominated first by engineering and manufacture, then by branding. The car industry now has to face up to a changing cultural, social and environmental landscape of increasing autonomy.

The first truly autonomous, full-size cars ran in the 1950s and 1960s in the US and the UK. Cables and detector circuits embedded in the road guided the vehicles, which were converted stock cars.

The 1970s and 1980s saw cars detach control from the road and read cues in the environment using cameras. By the 1990s, governments started funding new technologies with the potential to reduce traffic congestion and accidents. A number of vehicle manufacturers developed technologies such as night vision, active cruise control and lane departure warning, often in collaboration with academia.

In 2014, Google revealed its first in-house prototype, a small two-seater vehicle with friendly product design features rather than the sweeping curves normally associated with vehicle design. With no pedals or steering wheel, this was a purpose-built driverless vehicle – not a converted car. The same year saw another radical shift as electric-car company Tesla equipped its Model S with 12 ultrasonic sensors and a forward-facing camera to support autonomous driving.

Autonomous vehicles really moved into the public eye in 2015 with high-profile journeys such as a United States coast-to-coast record for a driverless car and several brands entering the arena. Volvo boldly stated that it would accept liability for any of its driverless vehicles involved in accidents and BMW launched an autonomous parking feature for its luxury models. Nissan prototyped an interior with 'driver' and 'driven' modes and General Motors and Toyota tested driverless prototypes. Tesla even updated its vehicle software to enable an 'autopilot' function, and non-car companies such as Chinese social network Baidu and mobility disrupter Uber also got in on the act and tested vehicles on the road.

Targeting older needs

At the Royal College of Art, we've been taking a human-centred approach to the design of autonomous vehicles, systems and services. As designers, we're working with people of all ages in teams including scientists, technologists, social scientists and others to find new solutions in this dynamic sector. Open source design and social media can enable members of the public to test solutions so that the design process becomes more democratic, moving beyond traditional vehicle design.

We have looked at social and cultural expectations, as well as fears, around driverless cars. It is important to reassure people that a car will make good choices on city streets and to prevent pedestrians from halting a vehicle by simply standing in front of it. Imagine the new possibilities as people and goods are driven around. Could hotels operate vehicles as mobile rooms, silently whisking guests across the country overnight? Or could a car be a mobile nanny, entertaining children and picking them up from school?

The driverless car is pulling up fast. It could bring enormous benefits to older people at a time of increased longevity and demands on healthcare and fewer people working to support those who are retired. Could it help mediate between the generations, taking grandparents to meet grandchildren without needing to negotiate a lift from parents? Could autonomous ambulances support patient transport and discharge, and driverless community vehicles bring much-needed services to a person's doorstep?

Whatever the outcomes, the driverless car has real potential to improve the mobility, access and visibility of people at both ends of the age spectrum. The intelligence is already there – we must make sure that inclusivity follows.

Rama Gheerawo is Director of the Helen Hamlyn Centre for Design at the Royal College of Art

Professor Dale Harrow is Director of the Intelligent Mobility Design Centre at the Royal College of Art

The world's first foldable wheelchair wheel was developed
by Duncan Fitzsimons at the Royal College of Art in 2007.
A wheelchair with this wheel can be folded up to be stored
easily at home, in the boot of a small car or in an overhead
locker on an aeroplane. Now in commercial production,
it is available from Maddak Inc.

project
Walk With Path
Lise Pape

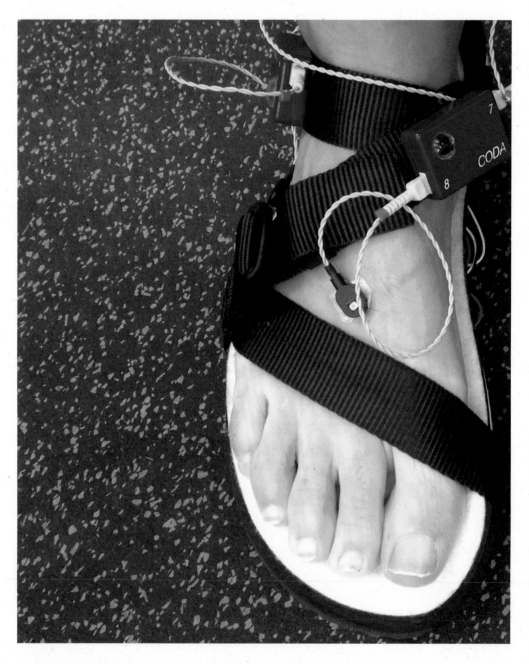

Winner of an AXA PPP Health Tech & You Award 2016
for independent living, Walk With Path's wearable products
reduce the risk of falls for vulnerable individuals. Inspired
by patients with multiple sclerosis and Parkinson's disease,
this insole technology provides visual cues to help the
wearer with foot movement and gait. Here, a prototype
is fitted into sandals.

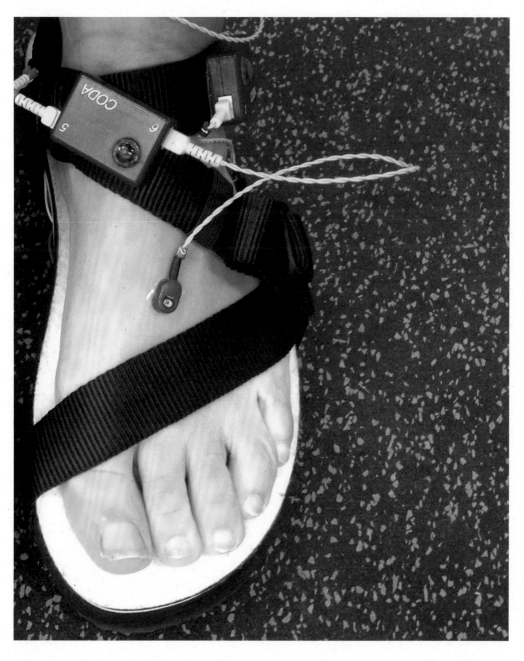

Led by the Transport Research Laboratory, this project
explores people's hopes, fears and aspirations around
autonomous vehicles. A series of design concepts represent
possible options. Based on an existing driverless vehicle
at Heathrow Airport (above), the project aims to prototype
new ideas in the London Borough of Greenwich.

First car　　White bike　　Mobility breakdown　　Talking to me?　　Security

Flexi pod　　Crashless　　Last ride　　Unresolved　　Secret Bionic cars

vehicle architecture　　Community pod　　Closer community　　What to do?　　Fast food

When we were commissioned to create a centrepiece about mobility for the NEW OLD exhibition, we immediately wanted to design a way to help people stay mobile for longer.

Designers have an important part to play in affecting behaviour. Over the course of many brainstorming sessions, we came to a number of conclusions. First, we wanted to design something for all ages – a product for life, a brand that could follow you through life as your mobility needs evolve. Second, our solution should be a product designed to help people stay fitter for longer and provide older cohorts with independence as their physicality slows down.

Push scooters are now ubiquitous in so many family lives. Every day, you see children on scooters on the school run, and parents riding them home. But at some stage, people stop using them. This may be because of stigma, safety concerns or simply the fact that older generations have not experienced push scooters in their younger lives, which creates a barrier to late adoption.

'We are people too'

During the development process, we held a number of research sessions with user groups, arranged by the Helen Hamlyn Centre for Design at the Royal College of Art. In one of these sessions, as we explored different ways of getting around, one user looked at a traditional motorized mobility scooter and exclaimed, 'You can smell the stench of decay on that'.

There is undoubtedly a stigma associated with mobility aids, and we were determined that our solution should address this. Many of the people we spoke to felt that current solutions felt like having 'one foot in the grave'. So we wanted to design something that was beautiful as well as highly practical. We discussed the requirements people had for mobility aids and came up with a list of boxes that our solution would need to tick: you had to be able to take it on a bus and into a shop, an apartment or a house, and there needed to be space to store groceries in it.

←↑
PriestmanGoode's Scooter for Life range provides practical support and stability

↓
Sketches capture the different life stages of the Scooter for Life

Indoor storage is particularly important from a safety point of view. At present, mobility scooters generally need to be parked outside the home, as they are often too bulky to be taken indoors or cannot be taken up the steps. This can introduce an unexpected safety issue. Parked in front of someone's home, a mobility scooter can highlight the fact that an elderly or less mobile person lives on the premises, potentially increasing the risk of crime.

Based on these key considerations, we developed the Scooter for Life, a product for all ages that is highly adaptable and helps older people improve their mobility in a practical way.

How it works

The Scooter for Life is designed to offer a reliable product and brand that can accompany you throughout your life, as your mobility requirements evolve.

Focusing on the benefits that it would offer older generations, a three-wheel arrangement (two larger at the front, one smaller at the back) would provide stability. A large front basket would serve the same function as a shopping trolley, allowing users to take their scooter into shops and providing a place to carry groceries while leaving their hands free. Users could also choose to add a small seat and electric power, allowing them to switch to electronic mode if powering by foot becomes too strenuous.

Using technology available today, a number of additional features would increase safety and usability. You could register regular routes, where the scooter could map the road and any unsteady sections of pavement. Other features could include a 'take me home' function, helping users with mild forms of dementia to get home safely.

On a practical level, the Scooter for Life could provide older users with more independence. On a societal level, it would aim to increase intergenerational interaction and counter the loneliness and isolation that many people feel in older age.

Throughout the development process, we also arrived at the idea of 'slowbility' – mobility for a demographic group that does not need to rush, that has time to enjoy the moment. The Scooter for Life would allow users to do that safely and comfortably.

Wider benefits

An important societal benefit of the Scooter for Life is that it would help tackle the 'last mile', the distance from a bus stop or train station to home. Not only would it present a more efficient way for people to get home, but it would also help on an infrastructural level. If you can encourage people to use their scooters more often and for slightly longer distances (around a mile), you could then extend the distances between bus stops, which would in turn allow us to relieve our over-stretched infrastructure and enable the public transport network to function faster and more efficiently.

136

Japan: designing a society for all
Keiji Kawahara

As a designer and educator with a commitment to 'enabling design' dating back to my time as a masters student at the Royal College of Art in London, I was recruited by the late Prince Tomohito to help establish universal design in Japan in the opening years of the twenty-first century. For many years, Japan has looked to the USA for industrial inspiration. It was therefore natural that in seeking to create a 'society for all' we should look there – to a place where universal design was leading the way.

However, with my links to the UK and in particular the RCA, I was aware that people in Europe were adopting a different approach, more allied to design and innovation. I was keen to open up thinking in Japan to ideas from both sides of the Atlantic. This process began with a conference I organized in Yokohama in 2002.

In the United States, the emphasis was firmly on creating a legislative framework that would oblige public and commercial buildings and services to accommodate the widest range of users. In Europe, the focus was around social inclusion, and in the UK on understanding the needs and aspirations of an ageing population.

All had facets relevant to the Japanese situation that informed and influenced the early activities of the International Association of Universal Design (IAUD) when it launched in 2003. The challenge, however, was to adopt these new ideas to the Japanese culture and way of doing things. It has taken time for a truly Japanese approach to emerge.

Traditionally, collaboration and harmony have been central to Japanese culture. These attitudes, along with the rapid ageing of our population, have helped shape design developments for older people in Japan by prioritizing empathy, kindness and consideration for others over pure functionality.

The goal is to ensure that our towns and cities, transport systems and public services are accessible to all, creating an inclusive and welcoming society in which all people can participate and contribute, regardless of age or ability.

Initially, the focus was on creating a barrier-free environment, in particular in city centres, but as our thinking is more directed at the group than the individual, we were concerned with the movement of larger numbers of people. Urban planning – especially around transport interchanges and social spaces – was more important than, say, residential housing. In parallel, important social values like respectfulness and consideration for others made it instinctive for us to think about 'considerate' environments and a service-centred approach to universal design that would eventually feed into our interest in robotics.

The other powerful driver in Japan was the demographic shift or 'super-ageing' of society, first seen in the UK, then in Scandinavia, and most recently and dramatically in Japan, which is now the 'oldest' society in the world. With this demographic shift come huge social and economic changes. For a country that has lived with a stagnating economy for some considerable time, unlocking a potential market for age-friendly products and services was a clear imperative that proved hard to deliver on at first.

The increase in tourism and the number of foreign visitors to Japan, which will reach a new peak in 2020 when the Olympic and Paralympic Games are staged in the country, was another driver. Recognizing just how 'disabled' Western visitors are when confronted with Japanese signage, and what a barrier the Japanese language and script is to foreign tourists, helped us realize that disability is to do with context as much as ability. This led us to concentrate a lot of energy on user interface design, language recognition, voice control and interpersonal communication, in particular, for hearing impaired people, and later across languages.

↑ →

Fukuoka City Subway in Japan, designed by Toshimitsu
Sadamura, set a new standard in universal design when
it opened in 2005. Its spaces and services are wheelchair-
friendly and each station on the system has its own colour,
wall material and unique symbol, making them easier to
identify for people with cognitive impairments.

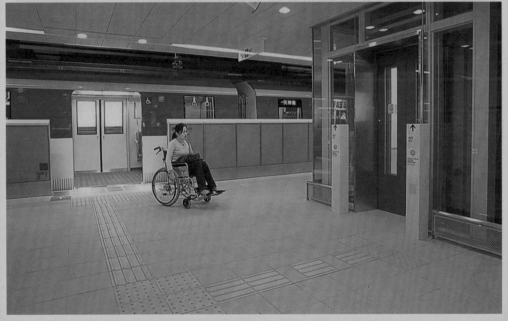

More recently, the devastating Great Eastern Japan Earthquake and Tsunami of March 2011 shifted our understanding of universal design and opened our eyes to the importance of safety and security, especially in emergency situations. Universal design is increasingly seen globally as an innovative and effective problem-solving approach to a wide range of social challenges, with its core value – engaging with the widest range of users in the design process – its greatest strength.

This broader understanding has become increasingly cemented in the design approach and brand strategy of major Japanese companies like Panasonic, Mitsubishi, Fujitsu, NEC Okamura and Sekisui, as exemplified by some outstanding entries for the annual IAUD awards.

For example, on the basis of extensive consumer research involving more than 30,000 households, Panasonic has created a new range of domestic appliances addressing the needs, aspirations and preferences of older consumers, with an emphasis on Japanese lifestyle and aesthetics. The corporation aimed to reduce demands made on users by making operations simple and intuitive. The success of this approach is demonstrated by a coordinated suite of products, including a washing machine, air conditioner, refrigerator, vacuum cleaner, steam and microwave combination oven, and a small rice cooker, each of which was recognized with a 2015 IAUD Award.

While focusing on consumers over 50 years old, Panasonic has applied universal design thinking to ensure that key features of this product range benefit a wide range of consumers, regardless of age and ability. With an emphasis on convenience, ease of use and operation, combined with reduced size and weight, the build standard speaks of durability and attention to detail, while the aesthetic is one of simplicity and timelessness. Although Panasonic's focus was to develop a range of products in harmony with the Japanese lifestyle, the resulting designs have the potential to appeal to a broad, international consumer base.

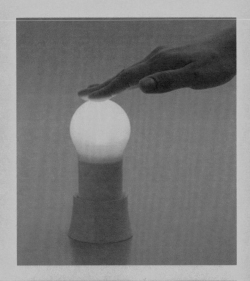

↗
LED lantern, an IAUD award winner from Panasonic, can be standalone, carried or suspended. It switches on or off with just a light push and remains cool to the touch.

↑
Paro the Seal is a therapeutic robot used to improve communication and reduce stress in dementia patients

In an extraordinary collaboration, Panasonic and Mitsubishi – companies that in other circumstances would see each other as major competitors – joined forces to demonstrate the benefits of voice-guidance technology for domestic TVs to people with visual limitations at a series of events. Not only does the technology benefit people with limited or no vision, it offers convenience for a wide range of users who have difficulty using a remote control, and is an important way of extending the accessibility of products and services.

Overall, the successful internationalization of this technology by Panasonic is a pointer to the potential market advantage of well-executed universal design innovations.

Professor Keiji Kawahara is Head of the Department of Design, Nagoya University of Art & Design, Japan and Executive Director of the International Association of Universal Design (IAUD)

Message from Her Imperial Highness
Princess Yoko of Mikasa

My late father Prince Tomohito was passionately committed to integrating older and disabled people into mainstream everyday life. Until recently, Japan trailed behind other developed nations in this regard, but my father was determined to rectify this and called on Japanese industry and municipal governments to join him in a radical initiative, which led to establishing the IAUD in 2003.

Today, IAUD counts among its members the majority of Japan's major companies and has extensive links with local authorities, universities and voluntary-sector organisations, as well as a global network of similar initiatives in Europe and the United States.

Universal design was readily and very effectively adopted in the fields of town and city planning, architecture and transport, but took root more slowly in industry. In the early days of IAUD, my father encouraged and cajoled the senior management of Japan's leading companies to engage with universal design.

Through a series of international conferences, design challenges, collaborative research projects and an annual design awards programme, IAUD has changed the perception of Japanese industry. This sector now recognizes a growing marketplace for considerate products and services in Japan's rapidly ageing population, and is beginning to develop a consumer offer with appeal across the generations.

In parallel, major companies have established in-house user research facilities, and design consultancies have developed effective collaboration methodologies. As a result, Japanese design, business and industry are now delivering the intergenerational and user-friendly products and services that an increasingly diverse and active society demands.

This dynamic initiative of my father's was beginning to bear fruit when he died in June 2012. It is with great pride in his achievements that I have taken on his role as Royal Patron of IAUD.

Norway: planning an age-friendly approach
Onny Eikhaug

Norway is a welfare state with a social model of governance based on ideals of equality and inclusion. Economists call this the 'Nordic model' – a stable economy where a strong public sector is combined with a productive and profitable private sector. As the Nordic model goes beyond meeting basic needs to look at protecting human rights and equality, this system of governance is particularly suited to an inclusive and age-friendly design approach.

According to our Prime Minister, Erna Solberg, the fact that we are growing older and living longer is not a problem – on the contrary, it is a sign of success. The Norwegian government's goal is to make our society more age-friendly, and to better harness the resources offered by older people in terms of their participation in, and contribution to, society.

This marks a paradigm shift, challenging the idea that policy on ageing is limited to aspects of long-term care. The plan for how to achieve this is presented in the government's strategy for an age-friendly society, 'More Years – More Opportunities'. This states boldly, 'We will update rules, counteract negative attitudes, reduce age discrimination, adopt new technology and provide better facilitation for activity and participation. Including older people in working life in particular will help secure future welfare, as part of the transformation Norway is facing.'

Design plays an important role in this strategy and is a driver for creating more innovative and inclusive solutions that enable everyone to participate in every area of society. This is recognized in the government's strategy for universal design. In 2005, 16 Norwegian ministries agreed on a binding action plan with key goals, measures and deadlines to work towards the vision of a universally designed Norway by 2025.

This ambitious vision is for all people to have the same opportunities to participate in society on equal terms, and to have access to the physical environment, transport, information and communication as well as other public services.

Inclusive and age-friendly design approaches function most effectively when activated at all levels – in local communities and business organizations, and via public services. The best practice projects outlined below represent a cross section of work that puts people first, meets social needs, influences business practices and achieves sustainable change.

St Olav's Hospital

Opened in 2010, St Olav's Hospital in Trondheim has received international acclaim and won several awards for its innovative, people-centred architecture, which brings nature, the city, employees and patients together in a non-traditional atmosphere. It is a great example of how universal design can benefit everyone.

The fundamental principles of universal design were established and prioritized from the beginning, involving patients and their families, various user organizations and employees. The entire medical district is open to its surroundings. Landscape architects adopted the patients' perspective by designing surroundings that facilitate treatment and rehabilitation. The hospital also incorporates tactile and natural materials, colour and an extensive art programme.

The university hospital only has single rooms, which all have doors that open on to a central workstation area. This has resulted in better sleep for the patients and a better overview for medical staff. Satisfaction levels are high among patients and their families, as well as hospital employees. The hospital has become an attractive gathering place for citizens of all ages, with outdoor spaces and parks for recreation, and a number of welcoming cafés and restaurants.

Bergen Light Rail

When planning for a new light railway in Bergen began in 2006, universal design was not a legal requirement in Norway. However, it became a guiding philosophy throughout the project, based on the experiences of various user groups – including older people. As a result, Bergen Light Rail is the first public transport system based entirely on universal design principles and is one of Norway's most successful urban planning projects since World War II.

↑
Facilities at St Olav's Hospital in Trondheim:
rethinking medical architecture

↑
User groups played a key role in the design
of Bergen Light Rail

The new light railway has made the old Hanseatic city of Bergen accessible for everyone, and passenger numbers have consequently grown more rapidly than expected. The comfort of the trams makes them more accessible for older people and those who might otherwise find travelling difficult, opening up the system for new users who might otherwise prefer different forms of transport. Bergen Light Rail has become the preferred method of transport for a large number of people, connecting neighbourhoods and enabling all citizens to take part in Bergen's rich city life.

Schandorffs Square

This project has created a modern, inclusive, age-friendly park in the heart of Oslo. Property company Höegh Eiendom AS owned a building on the north side of Schandorffs Plass, a public square comprising a dreary, grey car park that could only be reached via steps. Höegh wanted to develop the square into a neighbourhood park. The Norwegian planning and design standards for public spaces specified that it had to have good walking access, with no steps or slope greater than a gradient of 1:20. The height difference of seven metres across the site presented a real challenge in this respect.

Landscape architects Østengen & Bergo made universal design a key driver throughout the process. They worked closely with different user groups to gain valuable input and insights. They conducted slope tests with wheelchair users and researched and used allergy-friendly planting to reduce irritation to people enjoying the park.

Today, Schandorffs Plass is well used by many people living and working in the area and has been donated to the City of Oslo. People with pushchairs, bikes and wheelchairs meet there. The square is a compact, light and modern space that is also cosy and comfortable. This demonstrates that inclusive design in urban public spaces can be elegant and functional while meeting accessibility standards.

↑→
A dreary car park was reinvented as a public park in
Schandorffs Square, Oslo

Kahoot!

Norway's Kahoot! is today one of the world's fastest growing learning brands, based on gaming technology. Its games are played every day in more than 180 countries, by millions of people. Its success is based on a people-centred design philosophy that places respect for individual learning at the heart of its strategy.

A Kahoot! is a collection of questions on a specific topic, which can be answered in a group social setting on laptops, tablets or smartphones. The biggest ever Kahoot! took place in October 2015 in Oslo at Telenor Arena, where more than 3,000 older people learned how to use the Internet in one session. The event revolved around the idea of people becoming savvy digital citizens able to learn whatever they want, no matter what their age. This was a powerful symbol of universal design moving into new areas in Norway.

Onny Eikhaug leads the Design for All programme at the Norwegian Centre for Design and Architecture, Oslo

↑
Thousands of older people in Oslo learn how to use the Internet with Kahoot!

Arthritis: innovating for independence
Liam O'Toole

Arthritis is not just about aches and pains. It is about independence, confidence and living your life. Not being able to lift your leg above a certain height might seem like a little thing, but it may mean that you cannot climb in and out of the bath by yourself. If you have arthritis in your hands, gripping buttons or zips could be really difficult, which is the difference between being able to dress independently or not. In the workplace, stiff arms could make using a keyboard problematic, which means it could be very difficult to meet deadlines. We have also talked to many people with arthritis who feel that train stations, airports, banks and other locations are not laid out in an appropriate way for them, so they feel exposed and anxious about going out. Arthritis may not kill, but it attacks what it means to live.

It is not a niche health condition, and you are very likely to know someone living with arthritis – around ten million people in the UK are affected by arthritis or related conditions. Globally, it affects an estimated 1.3 billion people. And this number is only going to climb higher as our population ages.

Our work at Arthritis Research UK has already uncovered breakthrough treatments, and we are dedicated to uncovering new ideas to help people push back the ways arthritis limits their lives. We believe that innovative design has a huge role to play in achieving our objective.

There is a chasm between the inclusive design of products and public spaces that are needed to help people with arthritis live independently and what is currently available. Further, the design challenge is not just about functionality, but the aesthetics of what is available. For example, there are some aids and adaptations available, but people are resistant to bringing 'disability' or 'medical' designs into their home or using them in public.

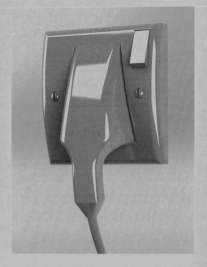

↗
Ezi-Plug, designed by William Dolman, aids ease of use for
people with arthritis in their hands. The socket switches off
automatically when the plug is removed. Arthritis Research
UK is supporting its commercial development.

↑
Peeler by Simon Kinneir, one of a range of kitchen products
developed to address the needs of people with arthritis,
in a collaboration between Arthritis Research UK and the
Helen Hamlyn Centre for Design, RCA

We spoke to one man who said that clothing and shoes are major obstacles to leading a normal life for people with arthritis. Since his hip replacement, he is unable to wear socks or lace up his shoes, but he finds orthopaedic shoes completely unacceptable, saying: 'I'd rather limp. No way am I going to wear that... If they made shoes that fit normal life, it would boost confidence.' He is not prepared to become so 'visibly' affected by arthritis.

There is a huge opportunity for the design community, and we are calling on designers to work with us to meet the needs of people with arthritis. We have already taken steps by partnering with the Design Council's Spark funding and support programme to help budding designers turn their ideas into commercial products. We looked for innovative product designs that offer practical solutions to the challenges of living with arthritis, and we discovered Handy-Fasteners: magnetic clothes fasteners that can be retrofitted to existing garments, replacing fiddly buttons, to make getting dressed independently much easier.

We have also been collaborating with the Helen Hamlyn Centre for Design at the Royal College of Art, looking at how design can help people with arthritis maintain independence. So far, this has included designing appropriate kitchen products, as well as producing a cookbook of recipes that prompts therapeutic hand exercise in the preparation of food. We are, of course, delighted to be actively involved in the NEW OLD exhibition.

And that is just the start. I want to see more design ideas for products and public spaces that address the needs of people with arthritis, but which do not carry a disability 'label'. I want the design community to understand the reality of living with arthritis, and the transformative effect that good, inclusive design can have on helping people with arthritis remain independent for longer. I also want them to see the very significant corresponding commercial opportunity. And, last but definitely not least, I want people living with arthritis to demand more from the design of products, services and workspaces that they use.

It is a lot to ask for. But I have always believed in the power of design to transform lives and address societal problems, and I am confident that it will deliver once again.

Liam O'Toole is CEO of Arthritis Research UK

↑
Handy Fasteners is a set of magnetic buttons that can
be retrofitted to any garment. Designed by Natalie English,
Matthew Barrett and Tom Fantham, with support from
Arthritis Research UK and the Design Council.p092

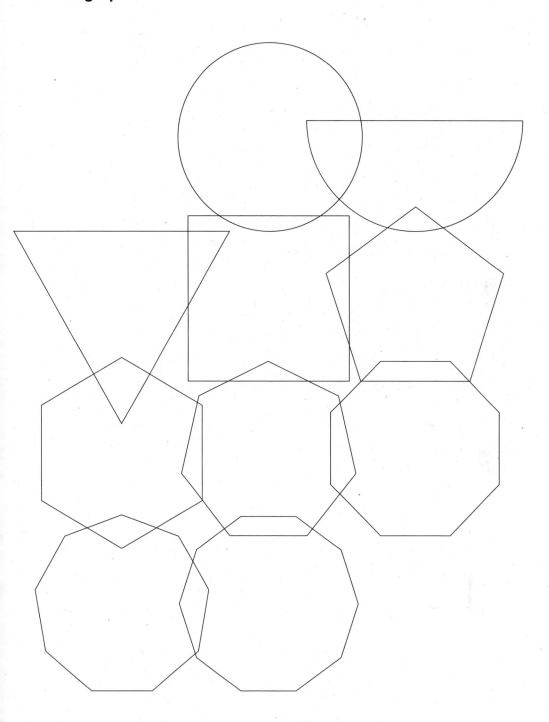

Yves Béhar/Fuseproject

Yves Béhar is a designer and entrepreneur who believes that integrated product, digital and brand design are the cornerstones of any business. In 1999 he founded Fuseproject, and remains its chief designer.

Over the past 20 years, Béhar has also pioneered design as a force for positive social and environmental change, and currently spearheads the SPRING Accelerator programme that supports entrepreneurs in East Africa. He has received numerous prestigious awards, and is the only designer to receive two INDEX: Awards for his work on the One Laptop Per Child and See Better to Learn Better programmes. Béhar was recently named Most Influential Industrial Designer in the World by Forbes.

Special Projects is a design and invention consultancy founded by creative director and industrial designer Clara Gaggero Westaway and experience designer and magician Adrian Westaway. Its mission is to enhance the unquantifiable aspects of life through conceptually rigorous work that blurs the boundaries between industrial, experience and interaction design.

    Adrian is a self-taught magician and full member of the Magic Circle. He is a tutor and lecturer in Design & Innovation at Queen Mary University and the Royal College of Art in London, and a visiting faculty member at the Copenhagen Institute of Interaction Design. Clara studied Industrial Design in Italy. She is a visiting senior lecturer at Queen Mary University and the Royal College of Art, and a faculty member of Oxford University Said Business School.

Future Facility

Future Facility is a new branch of London-based design office Industrial Facility, co-founded by Sam Hecht and Kim Colin. It focuses on giving form and meaning to the burgeoning world of Internet-enabled, technologically-driven products and services.

Future Facility's first project, the Oh! toothbrush with Braun/OralB, garnered industry interest for pointing to possibilities for everyday products in the new field of the Internet of Things. The studio's work has been well-received, winning more than 50 international awards, including six iF Design Gold Awards – more than any other British company. Future Facility's work is also included in significant permanent museum collections. Its monograph, 'Industrial Facility Works', will be published by Phaidon in 2018.

IDEO

IDEO is a global design and innovation company that practices human-centred design. Its researchers use ethnographic techniques to unearth insights into people's needs, while its designers translate those insights into products, services and experiences that people want.

Initially a product design firm that created Apple's first mouse, the first laptop – the Grid Compass – and the Palm V personal digital assistant, its remit has expanded immensely since then. Today, IDEO designs new products, services, experiences, organizations, ventures and systems with clients such as Ford, Nike, ConAgra, IKEA and the Singapore government. Through that process, IDEO helps its clients to build more competitive, resilient and creative businesses.

Konstantin Grcic

Konstantin Grcic was trained as a cabinet maker at the John Makepeace School in Dorset, England before studying design at the Royal College of Art in London. He established his own office, Konstantin Grcic Industrial Design (KGID), in Munich in 1991. Since then he has developed furniture, products and lighting for some of the leading companies in the design field.

Grcic has curated a number of significant design exhibitions, and has shown his work at solo exhibitions in museums around the world. In 2012, he was responsible for the exhibition design of the German Pavilion at the thirteenth Architecture Biennale in Venice. In 2016, he was invited by the German Design Council to curate the German contribution to the London Design Biennale.

PriestmanGoode

PriestmanGoode is a design consultancy whose work focuses on improving everyday experiences across transport, aviation and consumer products. Its expertise across a range of sectors has consistently enabled the studio to deliver new innovations, which have transformed the way we travel.

Over the past 30 years, the guiding principle in PriestmanGoode's work has been its belief that design is not just about styling, but about making things better and more efficient. The studio has become especially well known for its work in developing future concepts, visionary ideas to improve our everyday lives and encourage sustainable, long-term thinking.

Chairman: Paul Priestman; Creative Lead: Dan Window; Senior Designer: Mike Lambourne.

Jeremy Myerson

Jeremy Myerson is a design writer and academic. He is the Helen Hamlyn Professor of Design at the Royal College of Art, a visiting fellow at the Oxford Institute of Population Ageing at the University of Oxford, and director of the WORKTECH Academy, a global knowledge network on the future of work.

Jeremy co-founded the Helen Hamlyn Centre for Design at the RCA in 1999 and was its Director for 16 years, helping to pioneer the practice of inclusive design in response to population ageing. He is the author of many books on design and innovation.

He is photographed here by Dylan Collard as part of the Ages of Us project.

Deyan Sudjic

Deyan Sudjic is Director of the Design Museum in London. His career has spanned journalism, teaching and writing. Deyan was Director of Glasgow UK City of Architecture in 1999 and in 2002 he was Director of the Venice Architecture Biennale. He was Editor of Domus Magazine from 2000 to 2004, and was Founding Editor of Blueprint Magazine from 1983 to 1996.

Deyan has published many books on design and architecture, including 'The Edifice Complex' (Penguin, 2006), 'The Language of Things' (Penguin, 2008), 'Norman Foster: A Life in Architecture' (Orion, 2010), 'Shiro Kuramata' (Phaidon, 2013) and 'B is for Bauhaus' (Penguin, 2014). His most recent book, 'Ettore Sottsass, the Poetry of Things', was published by Phaidon in September 2015.

Deyan was made an OBE in 2000.

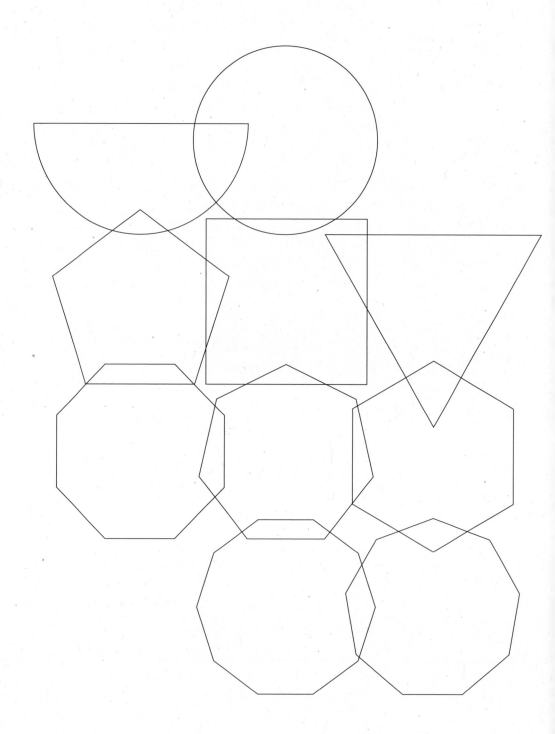

Acknowledgements

I would like to thank the Helen Hamlyn Trust and AXA PPP healthcare for their sponsorship of the NEW OLD exhibition, and Arthritis Research UK for its support for this publication.

Thanks should also be given to Ipsos MORI for undertaking a national survey on ageing, the Royal College of Art for providing valuable resources for the NEW OLD exhibition and publication through the Helen Hamlyn Centre for Design, Creative Review magazine for organizing its advertising challenge, The Age of No Retirement for sharing its network in intergenerational design, the Oxford Institute of Population Ageing and Government Office for Science for providing demographic data, and Roger Coleman for working with the International Association of Universal Design.

To the six design firms which have created speculative new projects for NEW OLD, and to the many individuals and organizations which have contributed ideas, essays and innovations, I am grateful for your creativity and experience.

Finally, special thanks to Helen Hamlyn, who first brought the subject of design for ageing to everyone's attention 30 years ago and has kept up the creative momentum since.

Jeremy Myerson
Editor

Image credits

Infographic sources

019
National opinion survey on ageing,
Ipsos MORI

020–021
Population projections by age
Office for National Statistics (2014)

026–027
'Predictors of Attitudes to Age
across Europe', Department for
Work and Pensions (2011)

044–045
'Ageism in Europe: Findings from the
European Social Survey', Age UK (2011)

064–065
'English Longitudinal Study of Ageing
Data', Department of Communities and
Local Government

084–085
The links between social connections
and well-being in later life, Department
for Work and Pensions (2015)

100–101
'Pensions at a Glance', OECD (2015)

118–119
Travel by age and gender, Office for
National Statistics (2015)

Credits

the Design Museum

Publishing Manager
Mark Cortes Favis

Publishing Coordinator
Ianthe Fry

Picture Researcher
Michael Radford

Graphic Design
LucienneRoberts+

Exhibition Design
Plaid London

Copy Editor
Lorna Fray

Editorial Coordinator
Margaret Durkan

Proofreader
Julia Newcomb

This book was published to coincide with the opening of the NEW OLD exhibition at the Design Museum, 12 January–19 February 2017.

Generous funding was provided by the Helen Hamlyn Trust, AXA PPP healthcare and Arthritis Research UK.

Royal College of Art

THE HELEN HAMLYN CENTRE FOR DESIGN

the Design Museum
224–238 Kensington High Street
London W8 6AG

designmuseum.org

First published in 2017
© 2017 the Design Museum
978 1 87 200555 3

Printed in the UK

→
Gerhard Kübrich, born 29 September 1913, Jena, Thuringia, Germany

←
Kiyo Aragai, born 10 September 1914, Sapporo, Hokkaido, Japan